TATIANA LUNGIN

WOLF MESSING

THE TRUE STORY OF RUSSIA'S GREATEST PSYCHIC

GLAGOSLAV PUBLICATIONS

WOLF MESSING
THE TRUE STORY OF RUSSIA'S GREATEST PSYCHIC

by Tatiana Lungin

© Tatiana Lungin, 1989

© 2014, Glagoslav Publications, United Kingdom
Glagoslav Publications Ltd
88-90 Hatton Garden
EC1N 8PN London
United Kingdom
www.glagoslav.com

Library of Congress Cataloging-in-Publication Data

Tatiana Lungin: translated from the Russian by Cynthia Rosenberger and
John Glad : translation edited by D. Scott Rogo
Includes index.
ISBN 978-1-78267-097-1
1. Messing, Vol'f, 1899-1974. 2. Psychics – Soviet Union –
Biography. I. Rogo, D. Scott. II. Title.
BF1027.M47L8613   1989
133.8˙092˙4– dc19
[B]

89-3154
CIP

Contents

FOREWORD 4

1. ENCOUNTER WITH A SEER 13

2. WAR COMES TO RUSSIA 18

3. LIFE IN MOSCOW 25

4. WOLF'S EARLY YEARS 31

5. FACING DEATH AND DESPAIR 46

6. THE LIVING CORPSE 55

7. STALIN TESTS WOLF'S POWERS 68

8. SOVIET SCIENCE "EXPLAINS" TELEPATHY 87

9. OCCULTISM'S DARK SIDE .94

10. THE ENIGMA OF MESSING'S GIFTS 107

11. IN THE ARMS OF MORPHEUS 125

12. MESSING SERVES AS A PSYCHOLOGIST 132

13. MIND CONTROL! 139

14. WHITE WATER ON THE VOLGA 149

15. WITNESSES SPEAK FROM AMERICA 157

16. THE BEGINNING OF THE END 166

17. PRACTICAL APPLICATIONS OF THE SIXTH SENSE . . . 172

18. THE CRISIS CONTINUES 184

19. NOTHING HUMAN IS ALIEN 196

INDEX 204

Foreword

Super psychic tested by Freud, Einstein, Gandhi and Stalin! That's the stuff of tabloid headlines bedecking the check-out counter. That's also part of the story of a remarkable human being, Wolf Messing, one of the four or five major psychics of the twentieth century, until now a man almost unknown in the United States.

Tatiana Lungin has side-stepped the sensational to create a warm, personal memoir of her long-time friend Wolf. Russians have a special talent for friendship, old-fashioned friendship woven together by little gifts of flowers, exchanges of keepsakes and hour-long walks to a friend's house for tea and talk.

Even by Russian standards, this friendship was an unlikely one. A teenager brimming with anticipation at the brink of her career, Tatiana first crossed Wolf's path just days before her world and everyone else's was irretrievably shattered by Hitler's Panzer divisions thundering into Russia. Messing and Lungin are survivors, and their paths crossed again after the war. This time friendship grew between the young woman and the mysterious, older celebrity who never lost the heavy accent of his youthful German. Eventually, she became his confidant. Now living in America, Tatiana has the freedom and the insight to show us both Wolf, the chain-smoking Polish refugee concerned about his family and friends, and Messing, as even he referred to himself when his great psychic gift was coursing through him.

Messing was as famous across the vastness of the Soviet

Union as rock stars are in the United States. Unlike rock stars, however, he was one of a kind. And his world was very different from ours. Just how remarkable his story is may become more apparent to an American reader by shading in the background against which Messing and Lungin lived and worked.

In the early sixties, the *Soviet Encyclopaedia* continued to inform readers that ESP and all things psychic were bourgeoise, capitalist fictions. "Anyone who promoted such fictions was accused of mysticism, something the state was pledged to eradicate. During the Stalin years, psychics were hunted down, imprisoned in labor camps or shot. At the same time Joseph Stalin, the man who had officially abolished ESP, was concocting his own ESP tests for a strange Polish Jew who had fled Hitler: Wolf Messing. Stalin didn't challenge Wolf with clean-cut lab tests. Instead he asked him to try a psychic bank robbery, or cast a psychic spell to breech the dictator's personal security forces. Even more paradoxical, while the few psychics and folk healers remaining lived deep underground, Messing wowed packed audiences with his mental and, to many observers, psychic powers.

With Nikita Khrushchev, a thaw finally came to Soviet life. In 1962 appeared a thin volume written by Dr. Leonid L. Vasiliev, an internationally known physiologist and holder of the Lenin Prize. *Experimental Research of Mental Suggestion* was an explosive book. Vasiliev revealed how he and others, at the government's direction, secretly carried on extensive parapsychological experiments during the thirties under Stalin. War disrupted the work, but now Vasiliev put out a clear, loud call for psi research to resume. "The discovery of the energy associated with psychic events," Vasiliev said, "will be as important if not more important than the discovery of atomic energy." It's a big statement. But apparently official ears were listening. Communist scientists — physicists, engineers, and biologists — swung into psi research.

The Soviet press, all official and all censored, began carrying reports of ESP; that made us sit up and take notice. We followed the Soviet media, tracking the increasing use of humor used to subtly criticize the government. Here, however, was evidence of a much bigger change. Even *Pravda* carried a from-page story about ESP experiments at the Newark College of Engineering in New Jersey. Funded by Chester Carlson, the inventor of xerography, this ground-breaking work involved telepathic communication that could be recorded on monitoring machines. The researchers, Drs. John Mihalasky and Douglas Dean, were friends of ours. Probably only about four or five hundred people in America knew much about these experiments, not because they were secret, but because, at the time, scientific psi commanded little interest. We read the *Pravda* headline in faraway Russia and realized *somebody* was interested.

We began corresponding with Communist psi researchers, trading articles and books and always tacking on a question or two, like, "Who are the best psychics in the USSR?" They answered, "This one in that lab, that one here," then added, almost as an afterthought, "and there's Messing of course." Messing, of course... The bits of articles sent us about Messing seemed to talk about a mentalist, a crowd-pleasing stage psychic. Why did the physicists and engineers accept him so matter-of-factly?

The mystery grew more tantalizing. *Science and Religion* — the party journal devoted to eradicating mysticism and insuring the growth of an atheistic, materialist philosophy — surprised its readers by publishing the first chapters of Wolf Messing's autobiography, *About Myself*, an outrageous story by anyone's standards. Here were tales of using the "power to cloud men's minds" to knock out captors and make daring escapes, stories of psi missions for Stalin, and accounts of how private citizen Messing had amassed enough money to buy and outfit two fighter planes, which he presented to the Red Air Force. In the United States wild tales in print are ubiquitous; but, especially regarding certain topics, they just don't exist in the USSR.

Ludmila Svinka-Zielinski — a seasoned Kremlin watcher and contributor to *Atlas*, the Western foreign correspondents' magazine — wrote about Messing's autobiography: "It is important to remember that under the conditions prevailing in the USSR anything done or written by such a controversial personality as Messing had to be scrutinized, criticized, and subjected to constant censorship, so that he could not get away with fraud... or anything that even approached a vain boast. In fact, we can be convinced that to survive and to exist in the environment on such a level, Wolf Messing must be thoroughly authentic."

We awaited the promised continuation of *About Myself*, but it never appeared. Messing remained a prominent question in our minds when, in the spring of 1968, we set sail for the First Annual International Parapsychology Conference in Moscow. It was the first and, so far, last such conference.

What about Wolf Messing? Scientists from all over the Soviet Union and the bloc countries answered favourably: he's genuine. He may not use ESP in every performance, but he has great talent and can do even more than his autobiography claims. He is *serious* — a high compliment in scientific circles. Things got blurry fast, however, when we asked the researchers how they knew. They hedged: he had promised to come to their labs, but he was old and so busy performing... It never came down to hard evidence; they told us Messing's ability was simply a known fact, and we should accept it. A few bloc scientists said they had run informal experiments with Messing, all successful, and confided the obvious: he had friends in high places.

The head of an Intourist office in Moscow talked to us about Messing's talent as if she were discussing the violin playing of Oistrakh or the dancing of Nureyev. "I've heard about Wolf Messing since I was a little girl," she said. She must have gone to see him a number of times then? Well no. "It's because I *know* he's so good that I haven't. I don't like the idea of someone looking into my thoughts," she admitted.

The magic of Messing's name worked with everyday Soviets, too, people of all sorts who liked to practice English with foreigners, particularly among the endless walking throngs that fill the city's streets and parks. Just about everyone knew of him. He was famous-a holy man, a hero, a legend. Occasionally, we heard fifthhand stories about his kindness, for example, how he helped locate a missing relative after the war; these are the sorts of stories Tatiana Lungin relates firsthand in her memoir.

Telephone books were under lock and key the USSR, unavailable to locals or foreigners, so we wangled Messing's number before arrival. "Yes, this is the home of Wolf Messing," agreed the woman on the other end of the line. We'd written about an interview, could he spare us a few moments? We very much wanted to tell Americans about his wonderful performances. She said she'd ask. After some time, she returned to say Messing had received our letter and sends his compliments. Unfortunately, he was somewhat ill from the rigors of his performances and couldn't see us at this time. He thanked us for our interest in his abilities.

According to Tatiana Lungin's account, Messing was probably under the weather. However, on that sweltering June day, it didn't take a psychic to know it might be less than politic to entertain two wandering North American writers involved in the parapsychology conference the authorities had just stopped dead in the middle — particularly as we had joined a greatly reduced number of Soviets to continue the conference under the friendly auspices of the Czech Embassy, a dissident, rogue embassy in those days only a few weeks before Soviet tanks clattered into Prague.

Messing the genuine, Messing the great talent remained elusive. Now his friend Tatiana has literally fleshed out the mystery. Reading her accounts of Messing's psychic feats, it's interesting to note how closely his specific talents matched the contours of Soviet psychology and particularly parapsychology, a field that evolved quite differently in the ancient Russian culture than it did in American labs, which relied on statistical ESP card-guessing experiments.

For instance, upon his arrival in Russia, Messing was put

to work performing amazing mental, not psychic, feats. This is squarely in line with a long, serious history of Russian interest in prodigies — people who calculate figures instantly, people who read pages at a glance, people with photographic memories, geniuses, and idiot savants of all sorts. The establishment, not the counterculture, spearheaded the pursuit of human potential in Soviet psychology. If one person can do such things, they said, maybe others can be trained to at least partially unlock such "reserves of the human mind." And stage demonstrations taught the public that the human brain was indeed a marvel — marvel enough to make the supernatural unnecessary.

Then there was Messing's cataleptic trance, his ability to put himself in a state of suspended animation. This quirky gift catapulted him from a street urchin's life to fame and fortune in Europe and the Far East. Catalepsy was another standing interest of Soviet psychologists, leading them to the intermittent study of yogis and, of course, to demand a demonstration of Messing.

Ideomotor activity involves tiny, unconscious muscle movements brought on by one's thoughts and imagination. By the time Messing tumbled over the border into Russia, Soviet scientists had piled up voluminous research on the topic. Such research fit the physical bent of their psychology and helped demystify some seeming wonders. No doubt, it was also seen as one more promising avenue in the ongoing exploration of the ways and means of mind and people control. Could a sensor on your throat pick up tiny traces of speech and reveal what you were thinking?

In 1950, the philosophy section of the Soviet Academy of Science was pressed to explain Messing. It was a bitter era; anything outside a very narrow norm could prove fatal. The ideomotor explanation must have seemed heaven-sent. The academicians declared that Messing was unusually sensitive to the micro muscle movements of audience participants who held his wrist as he moved about the hall performing. An official pronouncement, which Lungin has mercifully condensed in her book, was thenceforth read before each of Messing's shows, instructing the audience on all things ideomotor.

That Messing might have relied on ideomotor action for some of his feats is a plausible explanation. It is a highly implausible one for the more complex and whimsical challenges dreamt up by his audiences. It is no explanation at all for his ability to clairvoyantly see someone's besieged apartment a thousand miles away, or his ability to predict to the hour some indefinite future event that would occur.

Messing, in his autobiography, says flatly that the ideomotor tag was pinned on him by the cult of personality (i.e., Stalinism), and that it had no relation to his abilities.

The feat tying Messing most securely to the heart of Soviet psi research was his ability to influence the minds of others at a distance. Sometimes called telepathic hypnosis, this psychic spell is the Soviet psi experiment *par excellence*. While the tsars held sway, Russian scientists plunged into telepathic hypnosis, and Soviet scientists went right back to it as soon as the revolution ended. They showed off their success in a spectacular way at the 1924 All Russian Congress of Psychoneurologists at a Black Sea resort. A young woman waltzing in the arms of her partner, round and round an elegant ballroom, suddenly froze in midstep. A hidden psychologist had sent the telepathic command to halt — or so the scientific journals reported. Telepathic hypnosis, so foreign to American psi research, was the experiment endlessly repeated by Vasiliev and others in the late twenties and through thirties. They used it in part as a tool, a form of reliable psi, as they searched for the electromagnetic waves that carried psi. Ironically, they piled up the best evidence in the world that psi is not carried on electromagnetic waves. Telepathic hypnosis started up again in the labs of the sixties and continued in the seventies. Quite probably, it is still in some form being used today.

It's hardly surprising this was the psychic feat Stalin

commanded Messing to demonstrate on a grand scale, though surely not for theoretical purposes. His interest, no doubt, lay in the other aspect of telepathic hypnosis that had long fascinated Soviets: the ability to influence the mind and body of another person telepathically, usually without his knowledge.

A number of ESP abilities would certainly interest any dictator. Stalin may also have been intrigued by Messing's prophetic gift. Yet, he didn't appear to heed a prediction Messing made in a private Moscow club in 1940 that set the rest of the Communist elite abuzz. The Russo-German nonaggression pact was in full force. Messing, however, looking into the future proclaimed, "Soviet tanks will roll into Berlin!" The German Embassy quickly lodged a protest. After all, Hitler was still smarting from a 1937 Messing prediction of his ultimate defeat. The Soviet diplomatic corps huddled in confusion. At last they stated, "We cannot be expected to answer for the prophecies of Wolf Messing."

Again in 1943, Messing ventured to go public with a prophecy, risky for any psychic, but compounded in a land where psychics were not safe. The Baltic, Byelorussia, the Ukraine, the Crimea: all were in Nazi hands. The end of the war was not in sight. Messing himself had been evacuated to safety in Siberia. In Novosibirsk, the famous science city, Messing spoke to a packed audience at the Opera Theater. The war, he predicted, would end in May, 1945, probably within the first week.

Messing talked of various encounters with Stalin. However, he strongly denied circulating rumors that he'd worked with the police and intelligence groups. The Messing that Lungin knew was spiritually evolved — something that, contrary to popular belief, does not always accompany great psychic talents. He believed his gift came with a moral imperative: act ethically, help others.

You will read of the many ways he did help others, even though it was sometimes forbidden. In his autobiography, Messing mentions how he tried to help in subtle ways. His ability to powerfully implant thought in others, he said, could be used in an upbeat way to inspire people who were dangerously depressed: "I often succeed with forceful mental suggestion in giving courage, confidence, and strength to people who are ready to commit suicide."

Lungin remarks that Messing felt he would never be allowed to take a trip out of the Soviet Union. Dr. Vasiliev, the father of Soviet parapsychology, and other prominent researchers weren't allowed to travel either, not even to the satellite states. Maybe this is a sign of how seriously the Soviets take psi. Maybe, as Lungin suggests, there's more to it, and the secret remains locked away in the Kremlin. We still don't really understand talents like Messing's, nor the inner workings of the Kremlin elite, so, to borrow from Churchill's famous phrase about Russia, Messing remains an enigma wrapped in an enigma.

Happily though, we now have something to ponder and wonder about, thanks to Tatiana Lungin's memoir and her faithful record of Messing's comments. She has performed a real service for anyone interested in extraordinary lives, for Messing's story is full of the drama, improbabilities, and wild swings of fortune usually only found in Dickens. Anyone interested in human potential or, more particularly, in psychic phenomena will especially appreciate Lungin's contribution. Messing was a giant and deserves to be remembered in the West as well as in the East.

A long time ago, Messing made a seemingly impossible prediction. He told his young friend Tatiana that one day she and her son would live in America. Perhaps Messing looked even more closely into the future than he admitted and, then and there, chose his biographer. If so, like many other of Messing's actions, it was a wise and good choice.

Sheila Ostrander
Lynn Schroeder

1

Encounter With a Seer

The auditorium in Tbilisi, in the Soviet republic of Georgia, was packed to the brim with a well-dressed audience. The stage, starkly modest, lacked the traditional curtain. The decor consisted of two ordinary tables and several chairs. From time to time, the impatient audience clapped, anxious for the performance to begin. Finally, after the warning bell had sounded, a woman smartly dressed in black walked out onto the stage.

"Wolf Messing!" she announced unceremoniously. "Psychological experiments!"

The hall rang with applause, welcoming the man for whom they had been so impatiently waiting: Wolf Messing, a legend in his own time, a man shrouded in mystery. It was said he could read the thoughts of anyone to whom he spoke, locate objects hidden from his view, or spot a criminal on sight. Even more extraordinary was the rumor that he could take on the appearance of any animal he chose. Everyone, though, assured themselves that the state had forbidden such things, and that Messing had even signed a statement to that effect!

A few seconds after the stage director's announcement, a man of medium height stepped lightly onto the stage. He was middle-aged and wore a black suit that partly hid a snow-white shirt. His hair was extraordinarily long for those days. He folded his hands on his chest and bowed, while the audience greeted him with renewed applause. He walked to the edge of the stage, right up to the footlights, and I could distinctly see the gleam of a large stone in his ring. At that instant I experienced an intense flash from my past. I recognized this sorcerer as an old acquaintance; on the eve of World War II he had offered me a prophetic pronouncement. I knew I wasn't mistaken.

But my fleeting reverie was soon interrupted. My attention could not wander long from the performance on stage. The woman in charge that evening read some introductory material and explained that a panel had to be selected from the audience; they would be in charge of carrying out the "experiments." Six or eight people of varying ages and occupations were invited onto the stage, none of whom knew Wolf Messing personally. The panel began by sitting down at one of the tables and choosing a chairman. Meanwhile, members of the audience wrote down the most difficult tasks and questions they could think of for Messing to perform and answer. These notes were passed to the panel, who selected the most interesting and complex. Every member of the audience whose question was selected was then invited on stage. He or she would stand next to Wolf Messing, hold the psychic's left or right arm above the wrist, and impress the psychic's mind telepathically with whatever was written on the note. Messing usually carried out the task, after which the panel chairman read the note aloud to the rest of the audience.

Such an elaborate procedure was necessary for two reasons. First and foremost, it prevented the volunteer from falsely claiming that his task had not been correctly fulfilled. It also assured those sitting in the hall that Messing's performance had, indeed, matched the procedure written on the note.

Since I was so intrigued by what I knew about Messing, I wanted to participate in these experiments. Nervous as a little child the night before Christmas, I wrote down my request and handed the note to the panel. The jury seemed pleased with the task I suggested, and I was presently invited to go on stage. I walked up to the stage, barely able to restrain my excitement.

Then something truly startling happened. I approached the psychic and extended my arm to take him by the wrist; suddenly, he stepped back.

"I will not work with this woman," he said. "I know her. I conduct my performances only with people I do not know. There must be no suspicion of a deal. And I know her. Her name is Taibele."

The hall responded to Messing's speech with a round of good-natured laughter and applause. There was simply nothing for me to do but leave the stage, and I blushed all the way back to my seat. I was embarrassed and stunned by his memory, and, as the experiments continued, I recalled a series of events of twelve years earlier.

It was 1941. The bustling and good-natured citizens of Moscow rushed out in the evenings to cafés and restaurants, and to theaters and concert halls. Chess and domino players occupied the tables and gazebos in the city's courtyards and parks, while grandmothers strolled through the public gardens and avenues with their grandchildren and dogs. Russian visitors to the capitol and a few foreigners gawked at the unused but magnificent churches and temples. They drowned out the Muscovites in the stores, and dominated the museums and art galleries. No one anticipated the fiery and bloody war that would shortly come without warning.

It was a June morning. I sat in a comfortable leather chair in the lobby of a Moscow hotel, waiting impatiently for the director of a recently formed film association from central Asia to arrive. Outside, the summer sun grew intense, but the lobby of the hotel, with its marble floor and columns, was pleasantly cool and quiet. The doormen in their gold-braided uniforms created an atmosphere of palatial solemnity. I felt constrained and guilty. I was eighteen years old; in those days it was considered unseemly for a girl to be in a hotel, especially if she was unaccompanied!

The year before, workers from Soyuzdetfilm had come to our school to select students for bit parts and extras in a film entitled *Artek's Day* (subsequently released simply as *Artek.*) They looked at many students, and you can imagine my delight when I learned that I had been selected. The filming was taking place in the studios of Soyuzdetfilm, located on quiet Likhovoy Lane, sheltered near two of the city's famous landmarks — the Ring Road and the Hermitage.

My participation in this film became the most important thing in my life, though I still took great pleasure in school. The boys courted me respectfully, while the girls regarded me with envy. My instructors were impressed by my upcoming film debut, and the drama club even began assigning me the best leading roles. When the film finally came out on the screen, I saw myself against the background of a marvelous Crimean landscape, which I visited for the first time only many years later.

Now the film agents from central Asia were interested in me as an actress. I had no information concerning either the film or the role for which I was being considered. I only knew that I would have to go to central Asia for a considerable time to film on location. This prospect unsettled me somewhat, and my initial enthusiasm was already ebbing.

The hotel doors seemed to be opening and closing continually, and I eagerly examined every face that sailed through them. I had been waiting for thirty minutes, watching dozens of people coming in and out of the lobby, when one of these visitors emerged from the mass and drew my attention. This man seemed to hypnotically attract my gaze. He was wearing an expensive gray suit, a blue shirt, and large horn-rimmed glasses. His hair was slightly unkempt, reminding me of a shredded head of cabbage, and his nose didn't fit the rest of his face at all. It was too broad. His forehead was large and square, and his arms hung limply by his sides. I noticed that he clenched and unclenched his fists as though he had a nervous tic. Middle aged, very thin, and not very tall, he walked slowly and with obvious effort, and kept looking around. He seemed to be looking for someone. He moved toward my chair, stopped when he noticed me, and, now no longer looking around, headed right to where I sat. As he approached me I noticed his eyes: penetrating and ironic, slightly tired, but diabolically sparkling.

He gently smiled at me. "Ah, schöne Mädchen,» he said.

It was a little embarrassing to be told that I was a beautiful girl. Then, in rather bad Russian marked with a strong foreign accent, he asked my name. I told the gentleman that my real name was Tauba (which means pigeon), but that I was usually called Tanya.

«Taibele?» he asked again. «Little pigeon? Are you waiting for someone? Why are you sitting here?»

He closed his eyes slightly and dropped his head while listening to my answer. His lower lip quivered nervously and his eyebrows moved to the bridge of his nose; I could see heart-chilling anguish in his eyes.

«No?» he said loudly, almost shouting. «No! None of that will be!»

«What won't be?» I asked the stranger in a frightened voice.

«Nothing. Neither the film, nor the trip. *Nothing*. And for a long time!"

He spoke in the voice of a prophet — distinctly, syllable by syllable. His preemptive verdict filled me with a sort of mystical fear. I thought, this is the way sorcerers and magicians foretell disasters.

The strange seer said nothing further, but simply walked with the same slow and heavy gait to the elevator. I remained in my chair, dumbstruck.

Who was this stranger? Was he from the real world? Would I ever meet him again?

The film representative had still not arrived, but I no longer even thought about him. The words and eyes of the sorcerer who had just vanished preoccupied me much more for the time being.

2

War Comes to Russia

The war in Russia began a few days later. The fateful day Germany invaded the Soviet Union was June 22, 1941. Obviously, there was to be no filming and no trip for me to central Asia. The sorcerer's prediction had come true.

Just as with most unexpected misfortunes, World War II surged over Russia with little warning. Within just a few weeks we Muscovites were feeling all its adversities. Food disappeared from the stores, lines grew longer every day, a curfew was declared, patrols monitored the streets — everything indicated that enemy fire was nearing the capital. It all seemed so incongruous during summertime, when the suburbs of Moscow and the city's parks and public gardens are filled with the intoxicating scents and sounds of nature. But the war represented the only true reality, and I had to leave behind my rosy carefree youth. Now there was work to be done.

Until my unexpected screen "career" diverted me, I had from childhood dreamt of a life in medicine. The war strengthened my former goal, and I became a volunteer medical student.

We students were sent everywhere to help in the war effort, much entailing pure physical labor. During the summer we worked on collective farms, harvesting grain and potatoes from the fields and helping with livestock. In winter we worked unloading coal, wood, and other commodities from wagons.

I suffered hunger, cold, and physical exhaustion, but everyone else was in the same situation. We endured the horror for two years. But by 1943, things began to look better. The news from the front improved; the Germans were retreating. Victory, once merely a dream, now seemed like a real, though distant, possibility.

During the war, the Russian people laid aside their grudges toward Stalin's repressive government, their disagreements with the Soviet system, and even their personal problems. We all united against a common and terrifying enemy, our love for the Motherland uppermost in our hearts. From the very outset of the war, many people — especially the young — strove to be at the front.

When in 1943 the Leningrad District Military Registration and Enlistment Office of Moscow called for brigades of medical workers to be formed for the front, I was sent there along with many of my fellow volunteer students. We were under the command of military authorities in the wooded outskirts of Byelorussia (White Russia), from where German divisions had only begun to retreat. Epidemics of infectious diseases — including typhus — raged in the area. Since there was a severe shortage of medical personnel, I was appointed both deputy chief of the epidemiological station and head of the vaccination department in the town of Mozyr.

By the time we got there, the town lay in ruins. Ravaged even more than the city were the people's hopes and fates. The corpses of women, children, and old people lay everywhere in dugouts. I will probably never forget the starving baby girl who crawled around her dead mother, trying to suck at her cold breast.

The medical personnel were not only in charge of health and disease control; we were responsible for finding homes for orphans, cremating the dozens of decomposing corpses, and disinfecting all inhabitable dwellings. Each of us had to take on the work of three people, and rest was unthinkable.

Although the Germans were in retreat, they continued their bombing attacks at night. I was wounded in the leg during one of these raids. I continued working even after my recovery, and I was able to return home only after our group had taken final measures to control the epidemics. I returned to school, quickly made up for the lapse in my studies, and received my long-awaited diploma.

Peacetime finally arrived in 1945 with Germany's capitulation. Within a year I married and bore a son, Sasha (Alexander). Due to some unfortunate circumstances, I was soon left with the task of bringing up my child alone. This was extraordinarily difficult to do financially, since the medical profession is one of the lowest-paid careers in the USSR. So, I tried to find hobbies that could help me earn extra income. I had always been drawn to photography, and had often tried my hand at prose. After a long and tormenting period of indecision, I resolved to temporarily change my profession. I took a two-year course in journalism in Moscow, and was eventually able to meet several well-known photo-correspondents.

My first assignment as a photo-correspondent took me to Soviet Georgia to work on a documentary. My first stop was Batumi, a beautiful seaside town famous for its expert silver and copper engravers. My next stop was Tbilisi, the Georgian capital, where I was to photograph a picture story. The city's concert hall was only a stone's throw from my hotel, so, on my first free evening, I decided to get acquainted with Georgia's cultural life. I really didn't care what was playing that evening, whether it was a popular music concert or a classical play. But the hall's billboard announced the appearance of Wolf Messing — the man who could read thoughts. I had already heard a great deal about this legendary character, and I often dreamt of seeing him. I was lucky to get a ticket.

As I described in the previous chapter, it was here that I met Wolf Messing for the second time. Now, it was certainly not surprising that I recognized Messing when I first saw him on stage, but how could he have recognized me, and even remembered my name? He had uttered it only once some twelve years before. I also wondered what power lay behind his sixth sense. Was he a mystic? A clairvoyant? A mentalist? Perhaps he was simply blessed with a gift from God. This last idea sounded absurd even as I thought it, for in those days we all received an actively atheistic upbringing and few believed in God, other than old men and women still surviving from the tsarist days. Even they only professed their faith in private; you could get into trouble with the government for advertising such beliefs.

I sat through several of Messing's demonstrations that evening and returned to the hotel puzzled by what I had seen. Exhausted, I quickly fell asleep.

When I got up the next morning, the sun was already touching the tops of Georgia's mountains with gold. I went down to breakfast in the hotel's restaurant, gulped it down in a hurry, and was ready to leave when a quarrel between several men broke out behind me. The argument seemed to be over a pair of misplaced eyeglasses, which, according to the gentleman who owned them, were in the pocket of a waiter who was obviously elsewhere in the building. The gentleman's Georgian companions objected that they knew nothing about the glasses. Since one of the voices sounded familiar, I turned around. There was Messing! He saw me and took a few steps in my direction.

"Taibele," he said as if I were an old friend. "What a disgrace. They don't believe me. Me. *Messing.*"

At that point the head waiter intervened, and the dispute ended harmoniously. The eyeglasses were found precisely where Messing had indicated.

The fight over, the famous psychic took my arm and we walked out of the restaurant onto the noisy street. Our unexpected meeting brought about strange feelings in me. Everything seemed so natural, as if preordained, so I followed calmly. I felt as though I were obeying some confident and alien power.

A woman was waiting for Messing by the hotel entrance. I immediately recognized her as the master-of-ceremonies of the night before (for these performances she was called the "director"). The psychic introduced her to me as his wife.

"Aida Mikhailovna," she said with a smile as she extended her hand.

While directing her husband's performance, this woman had seemed stern, carrying out her duties without smiles or jokes. But now, I found her to be a pleasant conversationalist and an attentive listener. She was also intelligent and sensitive to others. Behind her sophistication, however, she possessed a magnetic simplicity. She knew how to deal with her husband, whose weak points I was to come to know all too well. His weaknesses, such as his temper, are such that claim especially those who are more attuned to the spiritual realms than we ordinary folk.

Since this was my first formal meeting with the renowned seer, I was naturally somewhat nervous. I was never unaware of the fact that he could read thoughts, so I tried to keep my mind occupied with neutral matters. You can imagine the result. As if to spite me, my brain cluttered up with all sorts of thoughts. I finally found what I considered a brilliant way of neutralizing my rambling ideas. I began to mentally "sing" a little song I remembered from childhood:

> *The priest had a dog, and the priest loved it*
> *It ate a piece of meat, and he killed it*
> *He killed it and buried it and on the grave he wrote*
> *That the priest had a dog and he loved it*
> *It ate a piece of meat and the priest killed it*
> *He killed it and buried it and on the grave he wrote*
> *That...*

You could sing this song for a lifetime without stopping. We walked for about ten minutes, with Messing in between holding us both by the arm. I sang to myself and everything seemed wonderful and peaceful, at least momentarily. Suddenly, Messing stopped dead in his tracks and turned to me.

"Taibele, aren't you sick of singing about that idiotic priest and his insolent dog?" he said. "Don't you know any other songs?"

If we had not been walking, I would probably have sat right down on the sidewalk. I was astounded by his telepathic ability. His wife seemed indifferent to the matter; she was evidently accustomed to such spontaneous displays. As far as I was concerned, something strange had happened. Although this incident shocked me, I calmed down and thought pleasantly only of the surrounding sights and sounds. This was how things remained throughout the years of our acquaintance. When around Messing, I was always calm inside, and no undesirable thoughts ever came into my head. The remainder of our morning walk went splendidly.

I still had work to do that day, but we agreed to spend the evening together; Messing was not scheduled to perform. We decided to eat dinner on Mtatsminda Mountain, a favorite relaxation spot for residents and tourists alike. The Georgians call Mtatsminda "Sacred Mountain." There is a magnificent park and a beautiful restaurant there, and a cable railway extends to near the 1,600-foot high peak.

At the center of the mountain is the sacred burial place for all renowned figures of the Georgian republic. We visited the site and were especially impressed by the pantheon. The great number of luminaries interred there was especially notable, and we were thankful that the present Soviet government had not cleared away the graves of the old Georgian aristocracy. Tradition had survived the revolution — almost. Alongside the graves of Georgia's many talented artists, poets, and actors, lay buried the "aristocracy" of the Communist party. Buried there is the mother of one of the greatest villains in all history, Joseph Stalin. Her marker is conspicuously taller than the others. Also in the pantheon is the grave of the great Russian playwright and satirist Alexander S. Griboyedov (1795 — 1829). In awe we looked inside the burial vault. The entrance is covered by an elaborate grille. By the small memorial stands a bronze statue of a woman with bowed head. The woman's face is not visible because a falling mantle covers her head, intensifying the figure's impression of mournful sorrow. This bronze statue is a depiction of Nina Chavchavadze, the poet's wife, and her words are inscribed on the tombstone: "Your fame will be forever in the Russian memory, but why did my love outlive you?"

Nina Chavchavadze was only twenty-two when she became a widow. Her great love for her husband only increased the pain of her loss, and she never remarried. She was destined to die quite young.

After our visit we climbed to the restaurant on top of the mountain. We didn't want to lose sight of the town, so we chose a small table on the restaurant's open veranda. The view from the mountain top is simply breathtaking; the cliff below is twined with the vines of wild grapes and various southern trees. We sat for a long time silently watching as evening fell on Tbilisi. Aida poured drinks for us, solicitously cut slices of meat for her husband, and mixed sugar into his tea. In the meantime, Messing sat helpless and weak, and seemed totally without initiative. He was obviously tired, which really wasn't surprising. While watching his performance the previous night, I noticed that he devoted all his energy to his psychic displays. He didn't seem to conserve strength for anything else. On stage Messing was consumed by a fierce tension, a state of both body and mind that often infected his audience as well.

Aida and I exchanged glances. No words passed between us, but we knew what the matter was. The psychic needed a sound rest. We took a few photographs and returned to the hotel; it turned out that we were staying only a room a part on the second floor. Wolf climbed the stairs with difficulty, which rather surprised me since he was only a little over fifty. His figure that night stood in stark contrast to his presence on stage, where he moved about quickly and energetically.

We spent the remaining days of our stay in Tbilisi together. It never occurred to me that I might be a burden to them. It took several months before we became real friends.

3

Life in Moscow

I tried to be disciplined, especially where my job was concerned. While working on photo assignments, I always attempted to develop my film on the spot. Now, performing this chore isn't always easy, and oftimes you just aren't in the mood. But, from a practical point of view, it can be a very useful procedure. For one thing, you don't return from assignments with poorly exposed film. You have the opportunity to duplicate your shots immediately, thereby avoiding any embarrassment back at your publishing house when it is too late. The following story is a famous one among Soviet photographers.

Oleg Knoring, one of the leading photo-correspondents for the weekly magazine *Ogonyek*, almost got himself into trouble when he returned to Moscow from a trip to the Far East. It was a costly journey, and Knoring did not develop his film on the spot. The film turned out to be defective. His job and reputation were salvaged only because Stalin himself was favorably disposed toward the photographer. Oleg had taken a flattering photograph of Stalin holding a small Uzbek girl (who worked as a cotton picker) in his arms. The photograph, technically executed, portrayed Stalin as a loving father to his children, the Russian people.

This story had long served as an edifying lesson for all the Soviet photo-journalists who knew about it — especially those who had not yet made names for themselves. Now that my own trip was drawing to a close, I started developing my film to be certain of its quality.

My work was interrupted by an urgent knock on the door. It was Aida, who asked that I drop by for a moment when I saw Wolf leave their room. Later I walked over, curious about the request. She had only managed to tell me that she was suffering from a serious ailment when Wolf returned.

"What happened?" he asked. "Do you feel bad?" He was so excited that he didn't even greet me. Aida didn't say a word, and for a moment there was tense silence.

"Aidochka, you must go to a specialist," Wolf finally said. "Don't fool around with this!" But his wife refused to listen.

Then Wolf made a pronouncement I would hear him repeat many times in the future: "This isn't Wolfochka talking to you, but *Messing.*" Wolf referred to himself by his last name whenever he spoke with his sixth sense.

The following day I accompanied them to the railway station. We agreed that our friendship should not end, and were about to say goodbye when the psychic and his wife suddenly remembered that they had not sent a telegram to a woman named Irochka. They entrusted this task to me, and I executed their request immediately. By this time I felt that something invisible united us. Perhaps I intuitively sensed that many years of my life would be spent in the company of these fascinating people.

I returned to Moscow that evening, and the next morning I turned my photographs in to my paper's editorial office. They were pleased with my work and gave me several days off, so I decided to use my little vacation to call my new friends. They invited me to their apartment for the first day of Passover. I eagerly accepted their offer.

I lived a short walk from Red Square, and it was necessary to traverse the entire city to get to where the Messings lived. They resided on Novopeschanaya Street, which, during the early 1950s, still lay on the city's outskirts. It took me over an hour to get there, but the walk had a tranquilizing effect. The lime trees dotting Moscow were about to bloom, the weather was favorable, and the walk seemed neither long nor exasperating.

The Messings lived in a three-story building that stood within the depths of a courtyard. With its well-tended flower beds, the scene reminded me of an ancient courtyard from an old Russian painting. I ascended to their second floor apartment, and found their front door adorned with a simple copper plate engraved with Wolf Messing's name.

The Messings' dog responded to the doorbell first, offering a rich but subdued growl. Aida opened the door, and directly behind her appeared Wolf's shaggy head. Their home was modestly furnished.

An ancient ironbound trunk, the kind that is fashionable today stood in the vestibule; above it hung a coatrack. Apart from the vestibule, the Messings' apartment consisted of only one room and a tiny kitchen. The narrow rectangular living room served as both dining room and bedroom. A large round table and a sofa stood near the far wall. It was clear they had seen better days. The only item of interest in the room was a large television set, sitting conspicuously on a tall stand. Televisions were a rarity in those days, and I later learned that this one had been a gift from the chairman of the Council of Ministers (the government's cabinet), whose son's alcoholism had been cured by Messing.

Next to the room's wide window, which occupied almost the entire wall, was a sofa bed upon which a gray-haired woman sat quietly. Her face was so youthful looking that her hair could have been taken for a wig.

"This is our Irochka, my older sister," Aida said as she introduced us. The woman extended her hand without rising.

"Iraida Mikhailovna," she responded as we shook hands.

So this was the "young girl" to whom I had sent the telegram from Tbilisi! She was going on sixty.

We became better acquainted. Wolf asked me about my work

with my paper, digging meticulously as usual, focusing even on trivialities. Aida bustled around as she festively and splendidly set the table in the spirit of true Moscow hospitality. I learned a great deal about the other "members" of the Messing family — their German shepherd, Dick, and their canary, Levushka. Wolf twice said, as if talking about a son or granddaughter, that Dick was raised aristocratically, and that he had paid one and one-half thousand rubles to have him trained. That was no small sum back then.

I also noticed that books were scattered everywhere. They were stacked in a bookcase, on shelves, even underneath the table and chairs. Despite the chaos, you felt they were treated with care.

Wolf was in a truly festive mood that night. Although an atheist by his own admission, he cheerfully celebrated all his religious holidays, as a kind of symbolic gesture.

The contrast between Wolf's professed atheism and his adherence to traditional Jewish rituals reflected the rift that ran through all Soviet society. Today, with the Gorbachev era's new emphasis on some degree of religious freedom, it is difficult to recall precisely how strong the social contradictions concerning religion were ever since the Bolshevik Revolution of 1917. By the time I grew up, churches, synagogues, and mosques had, for the most part, been converted into secular buildings, museums of religious artifacts, or even centers of atheistic propaganda. At the same time, it was quite evident that religious practices and beliefs continued to have a widespread underground existence.

Although the state frowned on such central religious practices as Judeo-Christian or Islamic marriage ceremonies, they were nevertheless performed and at least tacitly tolerated. A token number of Russian Orthodox churches, Jewish synagogues, and Islamic mosques were permitted to function. Priests, rabbis, and mullahs were officially appointed and, in their preachings, expected to implement Soviet state policy. Anti-Semitism was prominent during prerevolutionary Russia, and, although religious tolerance was incorporated into the Soviet constitution, many Jew continued to suffer from a social stigma that worsened in the last few years of Stalin's life.

Wolf's celebration of the Passover feast should be seen as a continuing socio-historical tradition. The annual festivity recalling the exodus of the ancient Jews from Egyptian slavery is one of the most joyous family gatherings to have survived thousands of years. Although there are slight variations each calendar year, Passover virtually coincides with Easter, and the Last Supper taken by Jesus and his disciples is widely considered by religious historians to have been a Passover meal.

We all sat decorously around the festive table. A separate and solicitous invitation was offered to Iraida. She got up slowly and with considerable effort, supporting herself on the arm rest of the sofa bed. She didn't move her legs, but rather dragged them, her whole body straining as she moved to the table. When everyone was seated, Aida served stuffed fish with dumplings and matzos (the traditional unleavened flat bread served at this festival). Everything was just right for a Passover Seder. Wolf put on a long white smock belted with a white cord, just as my grandfather used to, and read through the holiday service. We raised our glasses and pronounced toasts to Passover and to spring. Then Wolf gave a sign and everybody grew reverently silent.

"I hope, I am sure, that, at the Burdenko Clinic, Irochka will be *saved*!" He nervously shouted the last word.

"Is that the truth, Wolf?" Iraida's face lit up with hope.

"This is not Wolf Grigoryevich speaking, but *Messing*!"

This was the second time I had heard Wolf use this phrase," which by now sounded like an incantation. By referring to himself in the third person, he distinguished the two sides of his personality, and stressed the tremendous importance of his pronouncements.

Later, while helping Aida with the dishes, I could not refrain from asking a question that had long been preying on my mind: "How is it you're not afraid to be with a person who reads your thoughts?"

"But I don't have bad thoughts," she answered calmly.

I also wanted to ask about Iraida and about my host's own health, but realized that this was not an opportune time. It had grown dark and was time to go. I thanked them for their cordiality and the festive dinner, and went home.

4

Wolf's Early Years

Our friendship grew stronger as time went by. I noticed that the Messings were treating me like one of their own family. They shared their most treasured thoughts and plans, and often went clearly beyond the bounds of ordinary goodwill. I, in turn, tried to be equally generous with them.

A few weeks after Passover, the Messings invited me to an extraordinary family council, convened to decide whether Iraida should have an operation on her spine. It was now clear to me that she could not walk because she had a tumor. The family council was a mere formality; everything had been already decided.

The Burdenko Clinic was not only one of the most famous medical institutions in the Soviet Union, it was also one of the most elite, equipped with the most modern equipment and staffed by the most prominent specialists. It was no easy matter, as a rule, to be accepted there for treatment. You had to be a member of society's elite, hold a high military rank, or, at the least, be a prominent citizen. Even in the latter case, somebody had to pull the appropriate strings for you.

Nikolai Burdenko was one of the country's most talented and innovative physicians. Even during the most difficult years for Soviet science — the so-called Lysenko years, when dogmatism dominated research — Burdenko went his own way.

Trofim D. Lysenko was a biologist and agriculturist whose theories received Stalin's total endorsement and caused serious danger and friction among Soviet scientists. Stalin adopted the Lysenko doctrine — that characteristics acquired through environmental influences are inherited — and those who opposed this concept found themselves not only shunned within the scientific community but in some cases imprisoned, exiled, and even killed.

"Lysenkoism," as it became known, reached its high point around 1948, when it was officially endorsed as a scientific application of Marxist materialism. Originally limited to genetics, it quickly extended into areas ranging from plant culture to medicine. Just how risky any kind of opposition to "Lysenkoism" was can be seen from the proceedings of the Lenin Academy of Agricultural Sciences, which met on July 31, 1948, with Stalin's personal support. Lysenko's most outspoken opponent, Nikolai I. Vavilov, the Soviet Union's most prominent geneticist, was sent to a labor camp in Siberia, where he died during World War II. In recent years with perestroyka (restructuring), the Lysenko period has undergone extensive retrospective analysis, and such principled men as Vavilov have been recognized as martyrs of science.

Burdenko had remained on the fringes of the Lysenko controversy largely because his field was itself relatively noncontroversial, neurosurgery being part of the hard sciences. He was a pioneer in neurosurgery and also contributed materially to military field surgery. He achieved international recognition, being named an honorary member of the Royal Society, London. Burdenko, apparently through sheer luck or oversight, not only escaped Stalin's purges of the Communist party and of the armed forces that took place about 1937, but was in fact appointed chief surgeon of the army during that year.

You can imagine how nervous Iraida Mikhailovna felt the day of her operation. Since this was a spinal operation, the slightest blunder could result in her complete paralyzation. And the anesthesia had to be administered through a tube directly into the trachea. Even though the hospital possessed the most up-to-date equipment, intubational anesthesia was still something new in those years. Few knew the technique, and, more often than not, an ether mask was employed. Only much later did intubation using an oxygen, ether, and nitrous oxide mixture become standard practice in our clinics.

Luckily, our anxieties were soon relieved; the operation was a success. Wolf had already seen this outcome and appeared calm, but he had smoked continually in the waiting room.

I should point out that Wolf had nothing to do with getting his sister-in-law into this prestigious hospital. He opposed any sort of string-pulling, and never used his fame to benefit himself. He was too modest and shy for that.

We knew the operation had been a *technical* success, but this only meant that Iraida had survived the ordeal. There were no apparent complications. A *total* success, however, was contingent on whether Iraida fully recovered the use of her legs. We all shared the same thought as we gathered around her bedside sometime after the operation: would she be able to stand up? We soon found out. Although she was tired and awkward at first, she stood up! We returned home happy and content. The few steps Iraida took in the presence of the physicians and in front of our eyes were an inspiration. Messing's prediction had come true.

After dinner that night, the Messings and I sat around relaxing and talking. I learned that Iraida had been an actress while living and working in Leningrad. She had survived the Leningrad blockade and the death of her husband, whom she had buried herself. By the time the siege was over, she was suffering from total dystrophy.

While this is neither a book of history, nor a commentary on the events of World War II, the reader should be aware that Iraida's total exhaustion and malnutrition, together with her husband's death, represented a microcosm of the enormous tragedy of the city of Leningrad. Soviet historians are even now engaged in trying to fill out what they call the "blank spots" in the official version of the past seven decades. Among these issues is the cause that brought World War II to the Soviet Union, the Hitler-Stalin pact, leading to the division of Poland and the eventual invasion of the Soviet Union by Nazi Germany.

Historians are wrestling with the task of revising the history of the war with particular attention to Stalin's apparently confused and ruthless conduct of a conflict we then knew only as the Great Patriotic War of the Soviet Union — a conflict we knew only the tiniest fraction about. In retrospect, the German blockade of Leningrad, which caused the deaths by starvation of uncounted citizens, appears to have been a strategic certainty, given the rapid advance of the German armies and the unreadiness of Soviet defenses. Stalin assumed Hitler would, in fact, respect the pact the two men had signed. Historians now determine that there was ample time, transport, and logistical support to evacuate a large portion of Leningrad's population; in fact, the defense of that great city would have been far more effective if the armed forces had not had to allow for the maintenance of millions of men, women, and children.

As Soviet historians are now beginning to recognize, Stalin's insistence that Leningrad not be so "defeatist" created the problem. Its defense was undertaken by every last inhabitant, no matter the cost. This demand for tactically needless sacrifice ran parallel to Stalin's deep distrust of Soviet soldiers. In fact, when they returned home from German prisoner of war camps, they were promptly sent off to Soviet internment camps because Stalin maintained that — like the people of Leningrad — they should have fought to the death.

Thus, when Iraida came to Moscow physically and emotionally drained, she represented a human tragedy many times greater than herself. But none of us had the knowledge or historical perspective to understand that, as far as we can now judge, the death of her husband and her own suffering had been avoidable. After the war she came to live with her sister and Messing.

At four o'clock we seemed to have exhausted our conversational topics for the day, and I felt it was almost time for me to depart. Suddenly, however, Wolf lit up a cigarette and said, "Would you like me to tell you about myself?"

"But I know everything about you from Aida."

"No, not everything. What Aida says about me is one thing; another is what I say about myself!"

I was about to hear Wolf's story for the first time. Ten years later, Wolf used my notes of this conversation for his autobiography, *About Myself*. It is a fascinating narrative.

"I am a poor story-teller," Messing began. "But someday I'll have to try to tell about everything that's kept in this jar." He smiled as he tapped on his forehead. He pulled another cigarette from his pack with his long and bony fingers, lit it, and inhaled with obvious relish.

Wolf *was* a poor story-teller; he often jumped ahead or repeated himself. I had to follow the thread of his narrative with strict attention, just to catch its essence. I often had to ask him to repeat things, sometimes at the most interesting points. But he did not get angry, and repeated anything I didn't understand.

"I was born on the eve of the new century — September 10, 1899, in the small town of Gora-Kalewaria, near Warsaw," he explained. "At that time we were part of the Russian Empire. The life of the Jews living in that tiny town was hard, as it was, however, for many others. It was a monotonous existence, filled with fear, superstition, and struggle for pieces of bread, for a tiny place under the sun.

"I left home at an early age, and so I cannot relate everything about the life of our family. My father worked in a garden that did not belong to us, and he nursed fruit trees and raspberry and currant bushes. Even now I can clearly see the tender eyes of my mother, and my brothers with their gay and quarrelsome games. The visit of the famous writer Sholom Aleichem, then already an important figure in Jewish literature, was very memorable —

how could it have been otherwise!" He stopped momentarily and inhaled deeply on his cigarette.

"He hadn't come to make a special visit to our remote little town," Wolf explained. "He was only passing through. But fate granted me a personal meeting with him. He possessed a small beard, luxuriant moustache, and, most importantly, a kind, attentive gaze that emanated from underneath his eyeglasses. He patted me gently on the cheek, and, for some reason, declared that I would have a shining future. This, of course, was not the prediction of a prophet. Sholom Aleichem simply wanted to see a future celebrity in every Jewish boy. I never again had occasion to meet this amazing man, but, from that point in my childhood, I came to love him with all my heart for the great humanism of his books.

"Our family was religiously orthodox, at times to the point of fanaticism. Thoughts of God permeated not only the consciousness of my parents, but every insignificant step and action in their lives. They looked upon God as a demanding but just master of the destinies of men. Unlike my mother, my father did not spoil us with affection. He had a heavy hand that he was quick to raise. God forbid one of us went to him with a complaint! He did not like grumblers and whiners and could flog us mercilessly just because someone else had offended us before he had. He tried to raise us as rough and hardy little beasts, capable of standing up for ourselves in the hard and pitiless world.

"You understand, Taibele," Wolf said interrupting himself and turning directly toward me. "I unfortunately have no photographs in my possession — either of my father, my mother, or of any of my brothers. I lived in difficult times. My mother died of a heart attack with my name on her lips, and my father and brothers died violent deaths in the Majdanek concentration camp and the Warsaw ghetto."

With a clenched fist, he raised his cigarette to his lips. The diamond on his finger blazed with a feverish light.

"At six years of age I went to a Jewish school to study. The main subject in the curriculum was the Talmud, which had to be learned by heart. I had a good memory and managed this quite easily. My teachers even held me as an example to the lazier pupils. That is why they presented me to Sholom Aleichem.

"As a child I did not doubt the existence of God. Any other view seemed blasphemous, criminally audacious. The rabbi, noticing my early piety, decided to send me to the yeshiva to prepare for religious services and devotion. My parents were extremely pleased; they considered this a great honor. And the word of the rabbi was considered absolute. But I have to admit that I wasn't very pleased by such a turn of events. Why? I don't know ... perhaps I was tired of cramming, or maybe it was something else ... but I began to resolutely protest the destiny being prepared for me. They entreated me persistently, and when that didn't work, they beat me. But I persisted too, and finally they left me alone."

Wolf tapped on the palm of his other hand to adjust his ring, which had slipped awry. He continued.

"Once toward evening, my father sent me to the store for matches. Twilight was falling, and it was dark by the time I returned home. And here is where the first 'miracle' in my life occurred, the one that sealed my destiny. It was filled with meaning.

"On the steps of the porch, in the patches of fading sunset, a gigantic white robed figure appeared before me. Even now I can hear his words, spoken in a deep bass.

"My son! I am sent to you from above to determine your future. Become a yeshiva student! Your prayers will please heaven!"

Wolf grew silent, vividly recalling his childhood vision. After pausing several moments, he started again, but his voice was much quieter.

"It's difficult for me to convey the state I was in after my encounter with the mysterious giant. You must remember that then I was mystically impressionable. I must have lost consciousness, because, when I came to, I saw the faces of my parents over me, praying in ecstasy. After I had calmed down, I remembered what happened and told my parents. My mother shook her head sorrowfully, muttering something incoherent. My father, displaying admirable restraint and concentrating for a moment on some inner reflection, suddenly pronounced: 'So He wishes!'

"I was so strongly shaken up, and my father's words were so weighty and decisive, that I ceased to resist."

Wolf stopped again and asked for a glass of strong tea. He remained silent while the teakettle heated up, and he even seemed depressed. He stared into space, distracted. But several gulps of tea revived him. The creases at the bridge of his nose and on his brow smoothed, and his gaze warmed. I figured now was the time to stir his memory, to wake in his heart everything that had been repressed for so many years. But Wolf remained silent. Not wanting to rush things, I simply waited patiently. I examined his ring — a ring he never removed. Four platinum teeth held a broad, massive diamond of approximately three carats.

After taking a few more sips of tea, Wolf asked my permission to continue.

"The religious school was in another settlement," he explained. "For the first time I left my father's house to begin an independent life. Prayers, the Talmud, everything took place within the boundaries of the prayer house where I lived.

"Soon I was in for another shock. One of the religious pilgrims who often took shelter in our school was the 'messenger from heaven,' he who announced my calling in the name of God! I recognized him immediately by his enormous height and his unusual voice. I thought, 'So all this had been set up by my father!'

"That event shook my faith that earlier had been so deep. How could God have permitted this heathen to speak in His name! Now I believe that my father's deception was the key factor in my decision not to become a rabbi. From that moment I have been an atheist. Disillusioned, I left everything and set out for parts unknown."

He stopped suddenly and looked at me with a mischievous squint in his tired eyes.

"Oh, I completely left something out, Taibele. I forgot that, before I left school, I committed three crimes, one of which cannot be considered anything but sacrilege. I took vengeance on God knows who or why. I stole a collection box in which Jewish believers placed their donations for Palestine, broke it open, and took the contents for myself. My conscience cruelly avenged me for my deed. I became repulsive to my *own* self, having dirtied my soul over those miserable eighteen grosz — nine kopeks...

"With this capital I set off to roam about the world, or, more correctly, I ran away from school. At the time I was only eleven years old, but I understood that, from the railway station to where I headed, roads led in all directions. I reached the station so hungry that I couldn't resist digging up potatoes from a stranger's garden and roasting them in the ashes of a fire. This was my second crime against the commandments: I stole. While at the station I climbed onto the first train passing through, which, as it turned out, was headed for Berlin. There were only a few people in the coach, and therefore chances were greater of my being caught without a ticket. I climbed beneath the compartment seat, and there I slept. That was my final violation of society's laws. While sleeping I evidently stretched so that my legs struck out, and the first inspector passing by spied them.

"Without standing on ceremony he asked me for my ticket. I feverishly tried to think of a way out of the unpleasant situation. My nerves were strained to the limit, and I shrunk into a tight ball, preparing to leap away like some forest lynx. I unconsciously picked up the first piece of paper that struck my eyes and handed it to him. Our gazes crossed. How I wanted him to accept that dirty scrap of paper for a ticket!

"The inspector took it in his hands, twirled it around, and looked at me from beneath his brows. Still crouching in a little ball, I mentally suggested to him: 'It is a ticket … a ticket … a ticket …'

"The iron jaws of the ticket punch snapped. Handing the 'ticket' back to me and smiling benevolently, he asked me what I was doing under the seat!

"That was the first time my power of suggestion manifested itself."

The telephone rang inopportunely, for Wolf's story was becoming more and more engrossing. Aida picked up the receiver. The hospital was calling to tell us that Iraida had been placed on a somewhat less rigid regimen, indicating that she was improving. We were all cheered by the news, and Wolf and Aida decided to order food for the patient from the restaurant of a nearby posh hotel. They had lived in that hotel for close to four years and were well known there. They moved after the war when an extreme housing shortage struck Moscow; by personal order of Stalin, they were assigned their present apartment on Novopeschanaya Street.

By now my readers must be wondering how and why Messing managed to stay in the good graces of a man as sadistic and paranoid as Stalin. If we did not know it during the years we actually lived under Stalin, we are now learning more and more from contemporary historians just how ruthless and unpredictable he was. I have, myself, speculated long and carefully about the odd relationship between the infamous man in the Kremlin, Joseph Stalin, and the unique man on the stage, Wolf Messing.

For what it may be worth, Stalin's ruthlessness toward both real and suspected opponents was perhaps really caused by fear of unknown forces, elements over which even the powerful man had no control. In an unthreatening manner, Wolf Messing represented these forces to Stalin. If Stalin really felt that Messing could, for example, actually read his thoughts, and thus know his plans, he probably would have had him put to death immediately. Instead, Messing's gifts were baffling, awe- inspiring, but ultimately limited by his charming and unthreatening personality.

Stalin might have consciously or unconsciously seen, in the person of Wolf Messing, a way to tame, or even cage, some of the powers that held him in thrall. Let us remember that this self-confessed atheist, this ever materialistic Marxist, was a man brought up in what is now Soviet Georgia by a deeply religious mother, and schooled in an orthodox seminary. He turned from his early religious background and training to Marxist dogma, but he may well have retained a basic, and even primitive, awe of the supernatural.

Permitting Messing to participate in the perquisites of the Soviet elite may have been, to Stalin, a way of making certain that Messing's gift would remain "tamed" and not be used in a way threatening to him. They, and Messing, could be kept under control. Until we know a great deal more about Stalin's mental makeup, until the psychiatric records of the Kremlin's Medical Administration are revealed (if they ever are!), all this must remain speculation. Still, special favors, such as the separate apartment, indicate an unusual link between the two men. But now, let's return to Wolf's life story, as he continued to tell it.

"And so, Berlin!" he continued. "Earlier I had somehow heard that in the capital of Germany poor Jews stayed at Dragonerstrasse, and I searched out this street, where there really was a home for newcomers. I became an errand boy, and did the dirtiest work. I delivered things, washed dishes, shined shoes, scrubbed floors. I considered these the most difficult days of my hard life.

"Berlin overwhelmed me with its population and massiveness, and with the multitude of temptations requiring money that I, unfortunately, did not possess.

"Once I was sent to the suburbs to deliver a parcel. The effects of my chronic malnutrition finally made themselves known, and

I collapsed in a faint on a Berlin road. I was taken to the hospital, I was told later, without a pulse or any other sign of life, and was put in a morgue. I would have been buried in a communal pauper's grave but for sheer chance, or perhaps kind Providence. A student practitioner noticed my heart was beating, however quietly, and I was saved…"

The doorbell rang at this point, and we were again interrupted just as Wolf reached a climactic moment in his narrative. The German shepherd, who had been lying beneath the table listening to his master, was the first to rush to the door. Our visitor was a young woman, hardly more than twenty years old, from the Moscow restaurant. She handed a package filled with food to Aida. The Messings thanked her warmly for the speedy delivery; only an hour had passed since the order was placed.

"No, thank *you*, responded the delivery girl. "My mother works in the restaurant and has known you for a long time. And I'm a student at the medical institute. I've heard so much about you, but have never met you, and so I agreed to bring you your order with pleasure."

And with that, she left.

Wolf sat back down, but he did not return to his story. By now evening had set in, and as the Messings made plans for the following day, I bade them goodbye and left.

I walked back to the Byelorussian metro station, and although the walk took over ninety minutes, I did not notice the time. I paid little attention to the traffic, and did not feel tired in the slightest. The only thing on my mind was Wolf Messing. While he performed, Messing seemed alien to our familiar world of the five senses. His nervous energy transferred itself to everyone present, virtually electrifying the hall. But he was a completely different man at home: calm, affectionate, elegant, obliging, always ready with a joke. There didn't seem to be any connection between his stage persona and his real life personality. He was truly a man of mystery.

I attribute my obsession with learning the secrets that lurked within his mind to my youth. Many of the strange phenomena Wolf displayed would, today, bring out the numinous side of each of us. That is why I feel that it's essential for science to thoroughly and carefully investigate psychic phenomena. Maybe we can discover the factors that give rise to them.

It was a shame that the young woman's arrival had interrupted Wolf's story. I consoled myself with the thought that, sooner or later, he would complete it for me.

Besides these issues, I couldn't help wondering what was *physically* wrong with Wolf. Visible below his right ear was a tumor the size of a walnut. It was hard to believe he could be ill just like anybody else. I had first noticed the tumor in Tbilisi, and I'd since wondered if it would be out of place for me to tell him that his condition was nothing to trifle with. I could readily understand why he was ignoring it. Most probably his concern for others — his sister-in-law, for example — and his tight schedule distracted him from his own problems. Unfortunately, I couldn't voice my concerns as I was due to leave Moscow on an assignment.

When I returned from my trip, I learned that a new misfortune had struck the Messing household: Wolf himself was in the hospital! He agreed to have the growth behind his ear removed; luckily, there were no postoperative complications. When I visited him at his apartment, he was already up and around and seemed in full health.

"The operation didn't bother *me*," he said in a sarcastic voice. "But it will bother my audience. I know that many who attended my performances were convinced that I was able to read thoughts at a distance because of that little lump; that it served as a radio or television antenna."

What Wolf said was true. The most improbable rumors had been circulating in Moscow, and even in other towns, about Wolf's amazing abilities. Some people were convinced Messing had a special receiver sewn beneath the skin behind his ear that was capable of registering the brain impulses emitted by people around him. This operation had presumably been performed secretly in some foreign country. Other rumors were even more fantastic. Some believed that, for an enormous sum of money, a second layer of brain had been surgically implanted onto Wolf's original brain! The credulous folk who believed this saw Wolf's growth as part of a protruding cortex. Likewise, rumor had it that with the disappearance of Wolf's "suspicious" tumor, his unusual gift, could also disappear.

The only rumor with any truth in it was that a scientific organization located in a certain Western government did indeed unofficially offer a million rubles for Wolf's brain should the psychic die suddenly. This offer did not annoy Messing, who took a childlike pleasure in all the fuss made over him. He laughed heartily when he spoke of the curious offer.

"Well, no matter what, my brain will stay here in Moscow!" he told me after his surgery.

The operation had been performed by Boris Petrovsky, head of surgery at the first Moscow Medical Institute, who was then at the height of his fame; he had performed a multitude of difficult operations. His list of scientific publications was also commendable. Later, he reached the peak of his administrative career by becoming the USSR's Minister of Health.

Because things had gone so smoothly, Wolf was back to work in no time. He rarely conducted his psychological experiments in Moscow, but usually traveled to Russia's outlying districts. He especially liked to perform before student audiences, who were wonderful at thinking up complex and inventive psychic tasks. The National Performance Bureau, the government agency sponsoring Messing's performances, was especially well disposed toward the psychic's displays. They liked to use his gifts to promote their antireligious propaganda, believing that his gifts proved that even supernatural forces simply represented those inherent within the mind. Perhaps the forces were inexplicable, the bureau said, but they certainly weren't divine. They sent him to such areas as the Urals, Siberia, and central Asia where religious sentiment still throve.

It would, however, be unfair to say that Wolf appeared *only* in the rural areas of the USSR. His itinerary covered the country from one end to the other, including many major cities. He was received enthusiastically everywhere he went.

I was nevertheless surprised that Wolf himself constantly tried to convince his public that there was nothing supernatural or mystical about his powers. He continually stressed that he was an ordinary person, but despite his disclaimers, I am far from sure that he convinced everyone. Some people considered him a living saint. Wolf couldn't stand this type of adulation. But I suspect that his public attitude toward his gifts merely parroted the view of the Soviet government, which certainly didn't want Wolf promoting "supernaturalism." One hint was his open scorn whenever he was labeled a "performer."

"Is it possible that I'm a performer?" Wolf often asked me pathetically. "A performer prepares for his act. He studies and rehearses his role. He knows precisely what he will say and do. I don't act until I meet the subject. I have no idea what will be discussed, or what impromptu task has been prepared for me. Yet, I must enter the proper psychic stream with lightning speed."

It was truly a paradox. The National Performance Bureau could hardly have listed Wolf Messing on the books as: "Magician, first category, salary — 180 rubles for a magic session."

5

Facing Death and Despair

Seven years passed, and my friendship with Wolf filled me with increasing pride. At the same time, I had to be ever tactful with him, because he was a person of exceptional sensitivity. Wolf Messing was easily wounded. My son Sasha also became close to Wolf at this time, and he, in turn, took a liking to the boy.

I tried to make it clear to Sasha that Wolf was a person with an unusual gift, who therefore deserved to be treated with special sensitivity. I must give my son his due; he treated Messing with great respect without condescension.

Sasha had a rough-and-tumble childhood. Sometimes it seemed he had enough energy for three boys, and, when he released all that energy, he often upset me. Wolf was amused when I told him about my son's pranks, and persuaded me that the child would eventually become a sensible and honest person. Such praise from Wolf was, of course, balm for a mother's heart.

Sasha dreamed of becoming a doctor ever since he was a small boy, and Wolf ardently approved his career choice. I shared Wolf's enthusiasm and often spoke to Sasha about his future. I think that, in time, Messing and I managed to sow the appropriate seeds in the boy's heart. Sasha was growing up without a father, and Wolf tried to fill in the gaps by spending considerable time talking with him.

Those few years remain in my memory as a relatively quiet and peaceful time for both our families, but few lives continue placidly forever. Suddenly and when least expected, storm clouds appear on the horizon, oppressing the soul with pain and melancholy.

Wolf's personal storm occurred when his wife Aida fell prey to a malignant breast tumor. The clinic appeared in our lives once again, and there were more treatments and worries to preoccupy us. After her entire breast was removed, Aida required extensive follow-up treatment; no doubt Messing foresaw the sad but inevitable outcome. He became very depressed and there was painful tension in the family. Iraida Mikhailovna was occupied exclusively with her sick sister, and would sit at her bedside until late at night, fulfilling all the doctor's orders and those of Messing himself. The constant care eventually paid off, and the cancer went into remission… at least for a while.

I genuinely admired Aida. With what weapons did she arm herself for life? What spirit she had! In between chemotherapy treatments and radiation therapy, she accompanied Messing on tours and continued to moderate his psychological experiments. During a trip to the town of Gorky she fell seriously ill and, accompanied by a nurse, returned to Moscow by steamer. She was not even able to climb down from the steamer by herself and Wolf, gathering all his strength, carried her down in his arms. The Volga tour, thus cut short, was to be the last in her life. Her condition was so serious that she was given continual injections while on the steamer, just to get her to Moscow alive. This time Wolf did not put her in the hospital. With tragic clarity he understood that further treatment would be useless. He knew that this was the end of a story that had begun years before in Tbilisi, when he first told Aida her disease couldn't be trifled with. Aida also knew that she was dying, but even in such a condition her optimism prevailed. As she lived out her last days, she tried to convince Messing that everything would turn out all right. Her family created a completely peaceful environment for her at home, and no one entered the house without good reason. The nurse who had accompanied them from Gorky, Antonina Alekseevna Frolova, moved in. But, despite this serene atmosphere, life faded rapidly for her.

One day, Dr. Nikolai Blokhin and Dr. Josef Kassirsky visited the patient. Blokhin as director of the Institute of Oncology, a learned researcher, and the brilliant surgeon who had operated on Aida; Kassirsky, a blood specialist, was highly respected by Wolf. His friendship with the Messing family was social and not professional. Although he was a learned man with a worldwide reputation, Kassirsky, like so many others, could not explain Wolf's powers.

It was now the beginning of June, Aida's favorite time of year. The aroma of blossoming linden trees — many grew beneath the windows — penetrated the apartment after each rainfall. Both specialists sat in painful contemplation at the patient's side, as if guilty over their unsuccessful treatment of Aida's cancer. Also in attendance were Antonina Alekseevna and Iraida.

Later, so as not to tire the sick woman, everyone went into the small but cozy kitchen. No one wanted to leave; we didn't think it wise to leave Wolf alone to brood. With the inevitable death of Aida, he would be left in the world without a single living relative aside from Iraida. Wolf couldn't sit in one spot, and often got up to pace. Dr. Blokhin finally broke the uncomfortable silence.

"Dear Wolf Grigoryevich, you must not get so upset," he said. "You know, sometimes it happens that a patient is in a critical condition when suddenly an improvement sets in, and the patient lives for a long time in excellent health. I remember…"

Wolf wouldn't let him finish. He trembled, his hands shook, and red blotches appeared on his face.

"Listen," he said, almost shouting, "I'm not a child! I'm *Messing*! Don't tell me nonsense. She is not going to recover. She … will die."

He seemed about to collapse, but recovered himself and stood for a moment in the middle of the kitchen.

"She will die on the second of August at seven o'clock in the evening," he said quietly. He immediately grew limp and sank silently into his chair. I glanced quickly at Dr. Blokhin to catch his reaction. Stupefied by the sudden prediction, he bore little resemblance to the usually self-confident physician. His eyes registered both horror and respect at the prognostication and its probable fulfillment.

God, how I wanted Wolf's clairvoyance to be wrong this time! Oppressive silence reigned again in the apartment, and, as everyone parted, no one spoke a word. We shot each other parting glances, nothing more.

Messing's prediction couldn't remain a secret; it soon leaked into Moscow's medical and scientific communities. Blokhin probably told his colleagues about it. In any event, the seer's somber prognosis soon became widely known. No one wished for Aida's death, but a morbid curiosity had everyone in its grip. When July came, Aida's condition noticeably worsened, tension in the Messing household increased, and the days flew by more rapidly than ever before.

That August was different from any other I can recall. The first of the month is my birthday, but I could take little joy in the congratulations I received. I could think only of Aida and her husband's prediction. How I wished I could cross the next day off the calendar, to outwit both fate and time! Cigarette fumes pervaded the apartment, but, when I first entered the apartment, I did not immediately see Wolf. Finally, I spied him bent over the kitchen table.

The next morning I received an invitation to the Messings. He cried silently though death had not yet entered the house. The silence was palpable: it rang almost painfully in my ears. From time to time friends dropped by to pay what would be their last respects to Aida, and, because she was fully conscious, she thanked them for stopping in. No mention of her approaching end slipped from her. When evening set in, she began to talk more freely, clearly, and distinctly than before. Her requests became more frequent — I replaced the nurse who had gone home — and at six-thirty she asked me for a glass of water. It was to be her last request; at exactly seven o'clock, Aida Mikhailovna died. Death, as though a slave to the psychic's will, arrived to within a minute's accuracy of Wolf's prediction.

The three of us — Wolf, Iraida, and I — sat up silently the whole night in deep mourning. Wolf smoked countless cigarettes, sobbing and moaning hysterically.

Aida was buried August fifth in the Jewish section of Vostryakov cemetery in Moscow. All the appropriate religious rites were observed; Messing wanted it that way. The cantor was his friend. A multitude of friends and acquaintances attended the funeral. A few days later a fence was erected around the plot, and a black marble plaque was placed there inscribed with Aida's maiden name: Aida Mikhailovna Rapoport. From that time forward, every year on August second, seven o'clock in the evening, close friends gathered at the Novopeschanaya Street apartment to honor the memory of the wife, friend, and helper of Wolf Grigoryevich Messing.

After the funeral, Messing fell into a state of deep depression. It was beyond his strength even to pick up the telephone when it rang, and he had difficulty getting dressed or preparing a simple meal.

The situation was both ironic and tragic. On stage he could give dramatic orders to others simply with the power of his will. He could force his audience to carry out his every desire. But, when dealing with his own emotions, Wolf was powerless!

Wolf remained in this profound depression for nine months, and the silence that pervaded the apartment was oppressive. Visits there were painful ordeals, and it seemed that Messing would never be the same.

We tend to devote ourselves to many endeavors in order to make our lives both interesting and constructive; we devote ourselves most committedly to our careers and to bringing up our children. Such endeavors bring us not only psychological satisfaction and a feeling of usefulness, but help us to bear up under life's adversities. Through them we recover more rapidly from the illnesses and misfortunes we encounter along life's byways. Since Wolf did not have children, only one purpose remained: his beloved work. For the first few months after his wife's death, however, no one even attempted to talk to him about continuing his performances.

Wolf's sister-in-law had to take over management of the household. She was a willful woman with a dour disposition (she rarely ever smiled), and she was never able to express her feelings with regard to her sister's death. She instead tried everything in her power to return Wolf to life. Some six months after Aida's death she broached the subject of work. Wolf only winced painfully.

"I can't! I can't. I don't feel anything!" he responded, almost crying.

Despite his reluctance to continue his life, Iraida and I delicately returned to this suggestion daily. We hoped to instill Wolf with a renewed confidence in his sixth sense. After three months or so of bolstering Wolf in this respect, our suggestions — coupled with his own inner resources — finally elevated him from his despair. He himself began to speak of returning to work.

Not once during those many bleak months did I see any evidence of Messing the telepath. It seemed that his wife's death had vanquished his powers. However, his psychic powers were a natural gift, not the result of deliberate training, and so were only temporarily suppressed.

So it was that Messing finally returned to work. But there was yet another problem to contend with. Who would take his late wife's place conducting and supervising his performances? Wolf and Iraida offered this function to me. I was reluctant to accept; I didn't know if I had the stamina to appear on stage. I possessed the other necessary qualities and was devoted to Wolf, but in the end I turned down the offer because I was still absorbed in my work as a reporter. I would not have been able to travel with Messing on his constant tours.

Another factor complicated the situation: I now had a second son. Nature had not granted him to me; he was a gift of fate. While working on assignment in an orphanage in Baku (on the Caspian Sea in Azerbaidzhan), I became acquainted with a child who wanted me to adopt him. Vladimir became my second and elder son.

After my refusal, Wolf and Iraida thought of an old friend, Valentina Iosifovna Ivanovskaya, and offered the position to her. She completely fit their stage requirements: she was beautifully built and possessed nerves of steel — important features for Messing's assistant. She also had excellent diction. Although she was a perfect choice, it was still necessary to "show her the ropes" — to familiarize her with Wolf's protocols, and imbue her with some rudimentary acting skills. So, while Iraida prepared Valentina, Wolf slowly regained his own skills. Within a year, Wolf Messing was ready to appear before audiences in his full glory.

These developments took place while I convalesced in Sochi, a town on the Black Sea, following an unfortunate accident. Not long before Wolf's return to the stage, I was accidentally exposed to radiation in a uranium extraction zone in the mountains of TyanShan while on assignment. The hematologists I consulted prescribed immediate treatment at a seaside resort in the Caucasus, though they couldn't explain what benefit I would derive from the sea! Having always enjoyed complete physical health, this unforeseen illness overwhelmed me; I considered it unnecessary to tell anyone of it. I especially kept it from Messing, as it was so soon after his own grief.

The autumn season at the seashore had passed, but an Indian summer bestowed its benevolent warmth. Even at this time of the year it is still possible to go swimming. I sat on a hillock at the beach, thinking about nothing in particular, when suddenly I heard a woman's melodious voice.

"Wolf Grigoryevich, come over here," the woman said. "This is the sunniest spot!" Such a name could belong to no one else! I shuddered and turned around to see Wolf coming out of the hotel. We were delighted to see each other. The psychic introduced me to his new director. Her functions on stage were the same as those Aida performed — to introduce Wolf, explain the procedures, and give a running commentary. Her responsibilities were, however, actually much broader. She handled the negotiations for the performances, made travel and hotel reservations, and prepared Wolf's meals if they weren't eating in the local restaurants. They still had three days and two performances to give in Sochi, so we found plenty of time for walks and conversation.

Valentina suggested that Wolf bid me goodbye early the last evening; their flight to Moscow was scheduled to depart early the next morning. But Wolf said he preferred to spend the whole evening out walking with me in the warm, mild weather. We wandered along the Sochi embankment for hours. The delicately colored sunset changed to dark blue, the sea grew dark, and mists rose from the water. From the embankment we walked out onto the boulevard. Our attempts at conversation somehow floundered. Long ago I had acquired the knack of perceiving my friend's moods, and I could see that painful thoughts oppressed him. I decided to break the silence: I asked Wolf if he wanted to return to Moscow. "No," he firmly answered.

Only later did I understand the reason: his sister-in-law created a strained atmosphere at home, continually pressuring Wolf to devote all his free time to Aida's grave. Doubtless, the memory and the grave of one's spouse are sacred, but Iraida imposed monstrous demands, requiring Wolf to make daily visits to the cemetery, just as she herself did. This could not help but upset Messing's mental equilibrium.

In no way could Wolf be reproached for neglecting his wife's grave. Within a year of her death, he had a beautiful memorial erected to her memory. A white marble bust of Aida sat on a black granite pedestal five feet tall. Her soft, kind smile was preserved forever in the beautiful sculpture.

Here in Sochi, Wolf retreated from the nightmare at home. Despite periodic pains in his legs as he walked about, he wanted to see the world in all the glory he had been denied for so long. The sights and sounds of Moscow no longer delighted his senses; here in Sochi, everything seemed like summer.

The hours passed quickly. Though it was time for me to be getting some sleep, I understood that the evening must not be cut short. Wolf needed to unwind, even in my silent presence, and I did not want to leave him.

6

The Living Corpse

"So, i told you that I woke up among the corpses in the morgue," he said to me unexpectedly, as though no time had passed since he last spoke to me about his life. He spoke these words so quickly and indistinctly that I did not immediately realize to what he referred. Suddenly, it dawned on me! I couldn't believe it. Seven years had passed since he first, in just the same manner, began to tell me his life story. No normal person could retain such a memory, but Messing picked up his narrative precisely where he left off when the delivery girl interrupted him (see chapter 4). As we walked the Sochi streets, Messing immersed himself in his reminiscences.

"I am indebted to that student practitioner for the fact that I remained alive," Wolf continued, "but I was brought back to consciousness only on the third day by Professor Abel, a neuropathologist. I am indebted to him for something else: he deserves the credit for discovering my powers, with which you are now very familiar.

"I regained consciousness but was still lying with my eyes closed. There was a muffled emptiness in my head mixed with loud, disconnected sounds. Suddenly, someone's words 'appeared' in my head: 'This must be reported to the police, and then a shelter must be found for the boy.'

"I opened my eyes. A kindly looking man dressed in a white

gown was sitting on the edge of the bed feeling my pulse. It was Abel. In a faint and still weakened voice I said, 'Please don't call the police, and don't send me to a shelter.' The man's eyes grew round and his mouth fell open. But he composed himself. 'But did I say that?' he said.

" 'I don't know,' I answered, 'But you were *thinking* it.'

"Dr. Abel invited his colleague, a psychiatrist named Schmidt, to examine me," Wolf continued, "and I was given the simplest silent mental commands: open your mouth, close your eyes, raise your arms, and so on. The next day they conducted more complicated experiments. Schmidt's wife was my inductor, and the tasks were in some respects similar to those I do today.

"Dr. Abel spent much time working with me, searching for new variations of my telepathic abilities. He taught me to control my will and psyche, and taught me confidence.

"Later, Abel introduced me to my first manager, Mr. Zellmeister, a heavy-set man, cunning, ruthless and intense. Ensnaring me in a labyrinth of unbelievable quantity of contractual arrangements, he kept me firmly in hand, while pretending to be a benefactor concerned only with my well-being. The truth is, managers always mercilessly exploit their 'wares.' I, too, did not escape such a situation, since my manager always earned incomparably more than I did. But I was then without funds and friends, and did not complain about the turn of affairs. What I had known before was worse. Zellmeister sold me, as if I were his slave, to the Berlin Panoptikum, probably for a great deal of money.

"Now, this might seem unbelievable, but at that time people placed themselves on display as exhibits. The exhibit 'freaks' clearly understood that they were to be shown, for a fee, to a curious public. On the program at the Panoptikum was a fat woman with an enormous beard who exhibited herself naked to the waist. The spectators were even allowed to pull on her beard in order to convince themselves it was real. Siamese twins comprised another exhibit; they were sisters joined at the side.

They exchanged jokes, some quite bawdy, with the young people gaping at them. An armless man also entertained the gaping crowd. After deftly shuffling a pack of cards with his feet, he would roll a cigarette, strike a match, and light up.

"The fourth act, appearing three days a week, was the boy-wonder Wolf Messing. On Friday mornings, before the opening of the show, I crawled into a crystal coffin. When the spectators arrived I placed myself in a cataleptic trance.

"In the almost six months I was there, I spent half of my time lying in that cold, transparent coffin. They paid me all of five marks a day. This seemed like a fabulously large sum to a young boy accustomed to starvation and privation, but my dandified manager received thirty marks each day for me."

Wolf pulled a cigarette from a pack, lit up, and inhaled deeply. I was enveloped in a noxious cloud of gray-blue smoke, but did not dare say a word that might spoil his mood.

"The schedule gave me four free days a week," Wolf continued as he puffed away, "and I tried to make the maximum use of them by devoting all my time to psychological exercises. Every day I headed for the Berlin market and turned on my psychic sense, trying to penetrate the thoughts of the merchants. I tried to hear their inner-most secrets. Household worries, the intrigues of neighbors, dreams of eligible bachelors — the blonde heads of the young peasants and the respectable burghers transmitted all such information to me.

"But I wanted not only to hear their thoughts, but to verify the accuracy of my perceptions. I walked up to the market tables, and looked intently into my subjects' eyes, and said such things as, 'Don't worry, dear Gretchen. Don't think about it. Everything will be all right, trust in fate … Hans will return to you.' Cries of astonishment or embarrassed silences convinced me that I was right. I spent more than a year training myself in such a manner.

"Then my manager sold me to the variety show at Berlin's Wintergarten. This was a major stepping stone in my career: instead of playing the role of a living corpse, I could at least be myself. I appeared before the audience in two different capacities. In the first, I portrayed an Eastern fakir — something like a yogi. They pierced my chest with needles and ran swords through my arms and legs.

"At the end of the show an actor appeared on stage portraying a rich idler — a fashionable dandy dressed like an aristocratic millionaire. He wore a magnificent tailcoat and top hat, and his fingers were covered with diamonds. Suddenly 'robbers' would burst onto the stage and 'kill' him, after first stripping him of his jewels. After committing the evil deed, they became the kindest of philanthropists, distributing amethysts, sapphires, and diamonds to the spectators, and suggesting that they hide them wherever they liked without leaving the auditorium. Then a brilliant young detective appeared — Wolf Messing. He walked about among the spectators, passing from one small table to the next, asking the charming ladies and honorable gentlemen to return this or that jewel, hidden in such and such a place.

"This number was invariably successful, and the public poured in to see the presentation. But still I was paid the same five marks.

"When I turned fourteen, I again became an exchangeable commodity. This time I was sold to the Busch Circus, which was famous throughout Europe. I had already grown accustomed to this buying and selling process. I traveled throughout Europe with the circus. My employers, concerned about my popularity on stage, instilled in me the idea that success was the key to all good things in life. Nonetheless, I managed to find time to educate myself, and the greater part of my salary often went for tutorial fees.

"Time was on my side and I soon became quite a celebrity. My success relieved my manager of all financial worries, and he puffed up like leavened bread. But he was the first who, in point of fact, opened the doors of Europe to me. In 1913 he took me to the birthplace of Johann Strauss; this was my first serious tour. I began to perform at the Vienna Prater Amusement Park, and I can say without false modesty that I became the hit of the season.

"But this is not why beautiful Vienna is so memorable to me. All my life I will be proud of the friendships I made there. First, I had the good fortune to become acquainted with Albert Einstein. I confess that I was not even superficially familiar with the essence of his theory of relativity. For me he was famous 'only' as a world class physicist.

"Einstein had arrived from Zurich, where he taught, in November, 1913, after receiving an invitation to report on his recent findings to a convention of natural scientists and physicians. I don't remember for sure, but I think we gathered at Sigmund Freud's apartment because Einstein immediately introduced me to this no-less-renowned personality. I was proud and flattered to be presented to two such giants of science at one time.

"The apartment amazed me with its abundance of books. It is incomprehensible to me how one man could even lightly skim through such a sea of volumes in a single lifetime.

"Sigmund Freud's research was closer to mine in spirit than Einstein's calculations and formulae. But later, after becoming better acquainted with psychoanalytic theory, I couldn't agree with him on everything. I acknowledged the importance of his work, but I think he erred when he tried to apply his findings — based on his work with hysterics — to everyone. I especially disagree with his over emphasis of the libido. Freud was an important scientist, but he made mistakes.

"Freud already knew about my powers and proposed that we conduct some experiments immediately. He assumed the role of sender. I will never forget his mental command: go to the dressing table, pick up the tweezers, walk over to Einstein, and pull out three hairs from his luxuriant moustache. You can imagine my reaction. What could I do? I walked up to Einstein and explained apologetically what his friend wanted me to do. Einstein smiled and submissively presented his cheek to me.

Freud was pleased with the result, but did not try to interpret it psychoanalytically.

"After two years, Zellmeister told me that he'd planned an extensive worldwide tour. The itinerary extended over four years and encompassed such countries as Japan, Brazil, Argentina, and Mexico. The tour's kaleidoscope of events and visual impressions have become so jumbled in my mind that, when I try to remember them, I tend to confuse details.

"I returned to my hearth and home in Warsaw in 1921. Much had changed in eastern Europe during my leave. The revolution hit Russia like a hurricane, and Poland achieved its independence. The little town where I was born now belonged within its borders. I had turned twenty-two and was forced to enter the Polish army, but my service was strictly a symbolic one. I wore a soldier's uniform during my term of service, but I never once saw a firearm, nor did I have time to go through basic training. By the next year I was a civilian again. I didn't have to search long for my new manager, Mr. Kobak, a person totally different from Zellmeister in style. Mr. Kobak was a handsome man, who usually wore vividly colored suits and bright shirts highlighted by bow ties. He was always gentle and smiling. He was full of energy but didn't trouble himself running about booking tours. Instead, he handled the major portion of our negotiations over the phone in a thoroughly businesslike fashion. He was successful, too. Once more I began to travel through Europe, visiting new and exciting cities: Paris, London, Rome, Stockholm, Geneva, Riga. On this tour I tried to widen my repertoire. I was just as capable of getting bored with a set routine as anyone else. In Riga, for example, I drove an automobile through the streets while blindfolded by a large black scarf. I had no experience in driving. My hands held the steering wheel, and my feet worked the pedals, while a professional chauffeur seated beside me gave me mental instructions. He telepathically instructed me to turn, stop, move backwards, and so forth. Many thousands of people, who formed a solid wall along the sidewalks and roads, witnessed this experiment. They looked as if they were awaiting the arrival of a king or prime minister. This trick was performed as a publicity stunt. Since that time I have never sat behind the wheel of a car. Mr. Kobak and I also traveled to the other continents — to Australia, South America, and several Asian countries.

"I cannot help recalling an important meeting in 1927. We were in India at the time, and I managed to become acquainted with India's spiritual leader, Mahatma Gandhi. I had heard much about him as a statesman, and I was also familiar, through hearsay, with his philosophical views, though I never explored their subtleties. But, as an individual, he left an indelible impression on me.

"Gandhi, who was interested in my experiments, agreed to be my inductor. The task he gave me was very simple, but coincidentally produced an unexpectedly brilliant effect. I had to take a flute from a table and hand it to a stranger in the hall. The stranger turned out to be a professional fakir who always carried about a basket with a trained cobra. Then I gave him the instrument, one he invariably used in his performances, he could not restrain himself from playing a lovely Eastern melody. The cobra slowly and gracefully rose up through the basket's narrow opening. Admiration conquered my fear. The cobra performed a dance, no less graceful, precise, and beautiful than any a human being could do.

"In India I became acquainted with the life of the legendary tribe of yogis. I admit that I envied their capacity for entering a state of deep catalepsy for long periods of time, sometimes several weeks. My personal record was only three days."

Messing took a puff from his cigarette, screwed up his eyes, and glanced fleetingly at his watch. He smoked at every pause, including this brief respite.

"When I was in Poland, people would often come to me with personal requests. You can't imagine what I was forced to listen to! I never pandered to anyone's petty desires or idle curiosity.

I always governed my life by two principles. First, my help had to be truly essential. Second, the situation had to be of some personal interest to me.

"In Poland, almost everyone knew the famous family of Czartorysky counts. Besides appreciable wealth, they possessed a royal genealogy.

"In this family a banal event occurred: a diamond brooch that had been handed down as an heirloom from one generation to the next had disappeared. Eminent jewelers estimated its value at 800,000 zlotys*– a fantastic sum for that time. All the efforts of private detectives proved to no avail, and hope dwindled with every passing day. Soon the most unbelievable rumors were circulating.

"Count Czartorysky flew to Krakow** in his private plane to see me, just at the end of my performances there. He was very elegant and fashionably dressed. In spite of what happened in his house, he was in a good mood — not at all stressed. He was a true, mannerly aristocrat. He told me about the brooch and urged me to help if I could. We flew back to Warsaw that day.

"I should stop for a moment and describe how I looked. It will bear on the events that followed. I had long, curly, blue-black hair that fell almost to my shoulders. My face was pale. I wore a black suit, a wide, loosely cut cloak, and an imposing top hat.

"The castle, an enormous building made from red stone and built in the old style, had two high floors with endless halls, rooms, and corridors. Each room and hall had different colored walls and carpets, and was decorated with beautiful French furniture. A garden surrounded the castle; a fountain flowed in the middle of the park. Everything was very well taken care of. You couldn't imagine a better setting for either work or pleasure.

"The next morning I set about examining the evidence. Things were arranged so that everyone who lived permanently

---

* This would represent about $200,000. — *editor's note.*

** In Russia. — *editor's note.*

in the castle, or came there every day to work, passed before me. The Count readily introduced me as a fashionable artist from the capital to several people in residence: I met his wife, a beautiful Polish woman who was very proud of herself, and his daughter, who was also very attractive. I also met the maids and castle workers, dressed in special uniforms that displayed the family insignia. They all struck me as honest and decent people. I placed everyone beyond suspicion.

"There remained, however, one person about whom I could not say anything definite. He was a feeble-minded little boy and a completely inoffensive creature, the son of one of the servants. No one paid any attention to him; he had never been caught in any wrongdoing. No one suspected him at all, for it didn't seem he could appreciate the beauty or value of a diamond. He enjoyed total liberty within the castle and freely entered all the rooms. Although I couldn't pick up the boy's thoughts or moods, he made me apprehensive, and the feeling stuck in my mind.

"After some reflection, I decided to rely on my instincts. This case didn't require my sixth sense; I knew I could solve it rationally and psychologically.

"I remained alone with the child in the nursery, pretending to sketch in my notebook. I pulled a gold watch out of my pocket and twirled it around on its chain. Then, as if I had remembered something, I 'carelessly' placed it on a table and walked out. Through a window, concealed behind a potted palm, I observed the little boy alone.

"He immediately ran over to the table, grabbed the watch, swung it on the chain as I had, and shoved it in his mouth. He played with it like an ordinary toy for no less than half an hour. Then, suddenly, and with amazing agility, he leaped upon the neck of an enormous stuffed bear and opened its mouth. My gold watch glittered in his hand for a moment, then disappeared into the beast's open jaws. My instincts were right. I had not only found the thief, but his silent accomplice — the keeper of the stolen goods! Now, it was only a matter of performing an operation on the stuffed bear, and the mysterious disappearance of the diamond would be solved. When we cut the bear open, a pile of shining objects fell into our hands. There were gold-plated teaspoons, Christmas tree ornaments, and pieces of broken colored glass — as well as the Czartorysky family jewel. According to our verbal agreement, I was due twenty-five percent of the total value of the found treasure. Because the total value of all the things found in the bear exceeded a million zlotys, they owed me about 250,000 zlotys.

"I refused to accept this sum, but in exchange requested that the Count use his influence in the Seym to revoke their resolution limiting the rights of Jews. The Count gave his promise, and within two weeks the Seym abolished the statute."

Wolf Messing continued to puff away; he still wasn't ready to conclude his story.

"And there is another case in which a diamond figured," he continued, his memories flowing in never-ending cascades. "A handsome stranger appeared one day in a certain small settlement in a village near Krakow. He presented himself as an American interested in folklore, and he was busy writing down country tales and collecting old household articles. The villagers welcomed him with cordiality and respect.

"He fell in love with a charming sixteen-year-old Polish girl, and in a fit of passion asked her parents' permission to marry her. He presented the girl with a diamond engagement ring, and his offer was immediately accepted. In aristocratic Poland, the rich American seemed like a fairy tale prince; however, a vague sense of alarm disturbed the parents.

"As I happened to be touring through that region, rumors of my clairvoyance reached the parents of the young bride-to-be, and they came for me for advice. I asked them to attend my performance that night together with the prospective groom.

"I suspected that something was wrong the instant I saw him, but just to be sure I asked him several questions. He sensed trouble and immediately tried to leave the auditorium.

I cried out for the people to stop and search him. They tied him up and found a great many false passports on his person. An investigation revealed that he was a member of a well-organized band that provided beautiful young girls for brothels in Argentina."

Wolf looked at me with a guilty expression.

"Please, don't think that I, at any time, collaborated with the police, or with any criminal investigation agency," he said. "Wagging tongues have spread this sort of gossip more than once. No, I have never engaged in any sort of secret service work for personal gain, although I always answered their call for help if I could, without asking for anything in return."

I replied that I had never had such a suspicion.

"You be the judge of the next incident," he continued. He stopped for a second and smiled. "Once a very beautiful young woman visited my hotel room. She had white hair down to her shoulders and sky-blue eyes. She was thin and tall and wore a red dress with a kneelength hemline in a style that was very fashionable at the time. But listen closely; the rest will be in stark, unvarnished prose. Because of my fame and because I was a bachelor with all the attendant weaknesses, I always stayed in a first-class hotel on tour. This time my luxurious room was totally isolated from Mr. Kobak's room. I took one glance at the woman and understood everything immediately.

"'Sit down, madam,' I said politely, 'Make yourself at home. Such charming guests rarely visit the abodes of touring performers. I am extremely glad that you came. Have a seat, and excuse me for one moment while I order some refreshments.' Closing the door behind me, I took off like a shot to Kobak's room.

"'Run to the police this second,' I blurted out, 'and come back right away. Bring several men and come back. Don't burst into my room, but spy through the glass over the door. Fast!'

"I returned to my room and again began to shower compliments upon this beautiful woman. If only I could stall for time, I thought, just for ten minutes! Her dirty plan was as clear as day to me. My guest got down to business.

"'You perform such miracles. Amazing things. But do you know what I'm thinking right now?'

"'Forgive me, madam, but offstage I'm just an ordinary man. I'm absolutely certain that in such a charming little head there could only be charming thoughts.'

"'Who can tell? But I want to be your lover, right now, this instant!' she exclaimed and proceeded to rip off her clothing. She rushed to the window and shouted with all her might: 'Help! Rape!' I gave a signal that the show was over, the door flung open, and the police entered the room and arrested the woman. Obviously, I had been set up by some jealous rivals who wanted to ruin my reputation.

"Yes, Taibele, Tanya, Tanechka, there are so many stories I could tell you…"

He grinned in embarrassment, obviously aware that for the first time in many years he had called me by my real name — the name I had used since childhood.

He grew visibly tired that evening; he had talked to me for so long. His speech became rambling and incoherent. Under such circumstances, thoughts outdistance words. It was difficult for me to listen, not because the stories were long, but simply because I had trouble understanding him. Wolf did not speak Russian very well, and I had to concentrate fully. When I decided to write this biography, I fully realized how laborious and time-consuming the work would be. After all, I had to base my memoirs on notes constructed from Messing's accounts. My primary challenge was to successfully capture the "taste and aroma" of Messing's life, i.e., to preserve the essence of his thoughts and speech while paraphrasing his words in a modern language comprehensible to the reader. So, to tell the truth, by the end of this story I was somewhat weary. Yet I was afraid to interrupt him, and I tried to disregard my fatigue. Wolf was sticking to a strictly chronological account of his life, and I couldn't let such good fortune slip by.

The rest of the town had fallen asleep by this time, but every now and then we passed a pair of lovers on the street. Perhaps they were counting the stars. But since Messing was ready to continue his story, my thoughts turned to less romantic preoccupations.

7

Stalin Tests Wolf's Powers

Messing was ready to continue with his life story, so I thought it an opportune moment to tell him that I was making a permanent record of his narrative.

"Do you remember your first talks with me?" I asked. "Well, later I wrote everything down and typed it up. I'm saving it for the right time."

"You mean when times become worse for me?" Messing said.

"What do you mean?" I exclaimed, worried about the unintentional tactlessness of my words. "I want to publish my notes about your life and work during your lifetime. Or help you to do it."

"All right, Tanya, but only if you don't eulogize excessively, and write without . . ." Wolf grew silent for a moment, painfully choosing his words, "without this fog of mysticism. And you must let me look through your notes, or give me a copy."

"Tell me, how did you receive Soviet citizenship? Were you forced to take it?" I asked.

"You go right from psychology to politics," Messing said. "Yes, that period of my life was full of events both dangerous and tragic, as they like to say in Russia. It's amazing I'm still alive and talking to you now. Circus lions can safely leap through rings of fire, but no one ever taught me how to take such leaps.

"In 1937, during an appearance at a Warsaw theater, I firmly predicted that any German attack on the east would end in the destruction of Germany. I made this prediction before an audience of one thousand people. This prophecy cost me dearly. The fascist ringleaders occupying Poland placed a price of 200,000 marks on my head. It was no secret that Adolf Hitler surrounded himself with gifted psychologists and soothsayers from astrologers to telepaths.

"At one time a clairvoyant named Gausen worked for him, enjoying his boundless trust as 'court psychic.' I had seen Gausen's work. He was a full-blooded Jew and the son of a synagogue elder. Even though it was the reign of the Aryan, he was well received in all the leading salons of the Third Reich. It is possible that he correctly predicted the Fuehrer's first successes by reading the stars, but later, when his heavenly counsel began to foretell tragedy, his own star waned dismally. He was eliminated without further ado. There is an accurate and detailed description of his fate in Lion Feuchtwanger's *The Lautenzack Brothers*.

"The atmosphere of war was felt in Europe long before the first shots were fired. We all invariably hope for the best, even under the most desperate circumstances, and I, clearly aware of the brewing storm, tried to seek shelter in my father's home in the village of Gora-Kalevaria near Warsaw. Later, I understood that I would have to move to a large city. But even the secret Warsaw basement to which I fled couldn't serve as a reliable shelter indefinitely. Knowing the Gestapo was hunting for me, I decided to get out of Poland, which was occupied in 1939. And just when I was being especially alert and careful, I was caught. Walking along the streets of Warsaw, I was stopped by a Gestapo officer much taller than I. I figured he had followed me. The officer stopped me, looked at my face a long time, then pulled out of his pocket a piece of paper with my picture on it. I realized that it was a bulletin carrying a reward for my capture, and that Hitler's followers had posted it throughout the city.

"'Who are you?' he asked, pulling on my shoulder-length hair.

" I'm a performer...'

"'You're lying! Jew! You're Wolf Messing! You're the one who predicted the death of our Feuhrer.' I had indeed done so, in a Warsaw theater in 1937. The officer compared me with the photograph, then knocked me off my feet with a hammerlike blow. He lifted me up by my hair, squeamishly avoiding my bleeding mouth, and gave me a blow to the back of my head. He lifted me up again. My teeth remained scattered on the ground.

"I was taken to the police station and thrown into a cell without first being searched. While sitting there I realized that I had to get out immediately or die. With a price of 200,000 marks on my head, I had no doubt of the danger I was in. Everything had to be resolved before morning, but I wasn't afraid.

"Focusing my will, I hypnotically compelled the police guards outside the building to join their colleagues inside. Then I compelled all the police on the premises to gather in my cell, telepathically, suggesting to them that they were entering an empty cell. I can't say exactly how many there were — at least nine or ten. Their expressions were very angry, and, to me, they all looked like kin. They talked about me (they said *they* were much stronger than my telepathy), but paid absolutely no attention to me. I hypnotized each guard, compelling them to stay in the cell.

"I remained perfectly still, afraid to make the slightest noise; I couldn't depend solely on my psychic prowess. So, like a tiny mouse sneaking past a hungry cat, I crept past the police as they continued joking.

"I breathed a sigh of relief only when the bolt on the ironbound door fell into place behind me, and I no longer had to fear an immediate chase. I can imagine the commotion that took place twenty minutes later, when they were due to be released from their trance! They would discover themselves locked in their own prison cell. But I still had to make my way to refuge, maybe find some kindhearted people in Warsaw, which, since it was now nightfall, had become doubly dangerous for me. A strict curfew was in effect, and I could be detained on the slightest grounds. If my trick in the police station became known, I would never live to morning.

"But the world is not without good people. I maneuvered through block after block in the darkness of Warsaw's deserted alleyways, until I found myself in a suburb. The cheap furnished rooms in this section sheltered unsuccessful actors, alcoholic artists, and aging prostitutes. It was an area the Germans searched only in daylight.

"I had never been in this area before, but I distinctly remembered the address of an old, kindhearted Hungarian circus clown named Janos I had met touring through Austria. While parodying the performance of an aerial gymnast, he fell from the trapeze wire. That performance was his last. In prewar years he lived primarily on charity, including donations from the Actors' Guild. Twice I mailed him money, but I never visited his apartment. I had no doubt that Janos would give me shelter, regardless of personal risk, and that's the way it turned out. I spent two days at his apartment without once setting foot outside. During the day Janos went to buy food and, on my instructions, collected money and valuables that I had hoarded away.

"I had to leave Poland and make my way cast. In those days, many people were convinced that they could find safety from fascism in the Soviet Union, and I was no exception. Before dawn on the third day, a peasant cart filled with hay stopped in front of the house. A softhearted Pole carried me out of Warsaw in this cart. Janos had made the arrangement with him at the market the previous evening.

"Once outside the city I was passed from one escort to another. I paid them both generously with the valuables I had taken with me, and within a week reached the shores of the Western Bug River.

"The bow of the small boat I hired struck lightly against a sand bar in the river, but finally I crossed the Rubicon.

Navigating only by the stars, I kept a direct course for the east, avoiding any border posts. I was unfamiliar with the area and with the customs of this new country, and I had to blend in with the stream of refugees. Finally I made it to Brest, where I immediately presented myself to the authorities.

"At first this new world seemed strange and unusual. Russia was harsh yet sentimental, bustling yet sluggish to the point of drowsiness. I was struck by these extremes. The fact that I barely spoke the language also posed a problem, and I quite frequently got myself into some amusing situations. The red tape involved in processing my documents went smoothly enough, but the enormous influx of refugees made it impossible to find tolerable housing. I was left to deal with this problem on my own. In western Europe, I would have easily resolved this by going to a hotel. But none of my offers to pay even triple the rate for a room had any effect, and I was told everywhere I went that there were simply no vacancies. So, I was forced to spend my first night in the USSR in a synagogue. I never lost heart, though, and considered myself a pilgrim just arriving after a long journey to Mecca. I decided to go to the cultural affairs department of the local municipality, which greeted me politely but with reserve. Representatives from the supernatural professions — fortunetellers, seers, telepaths, and parapsychologists — have never been welcome in the Soviet Union, and so it is even to this day. I spent a long time convincing them that my experiments were far from being some sort of charlatan or side-show performances, and I willingly demonstrated my powers to the skeptics. The coldness and even animosity I often encountered would interfere with my work in the future.

"At last, the cultural affairs department agreed to include me with a brigade of artists touring the Brest region. Things were getting better, only I continually got myself into trouble because of my poor Russian. When arranging the sequence of the acts for the performance, the director once instructed: 'Give him the *last* act on the program.'

"My vanity got the best of me, and I protested almost irritably: 'But I'm the best telepath in the world! Why am I the last?'

"In general, I can't say that life was hard for me then. My touring companions treated me respectfully and gradually initiated me into my new life. There was no money grubbing, squabbling, or jealousy among members of the troupe, a rare phenomenon on more provincial stages. The troupe worked out of love for their art, and were satisfied with small rewards.

"For the first time I had occasion to taste the propaganda imbuing the art of my new motherland. I marched in the ranks of the intelligentsia and workers of culture in a May Day demonstration in 1940, one year before Russia entered the war, and was entrusted with the most honored poster — a portrait of Joseph Stalin, 'father of the people.' But I was soon transferred to Minsk, capital of Byelorussia, where my performances attracted the interest of high authorities.

"Here I was presented to the secretary of the republic's Central Committee, Panteleymon Kondratyevich Ponomarenko, who later became leader of the partisan detachments in Byelorussia. When the war ended he became a member of the Politburo in Moscow. Evidently, he considered it necessary to report on my activities to Stalin himself.

"Once, when I was performing in a club in Gomel, two KGB officers entered the hall. They unceremoniously interrupted the act, apologized to the spectators, and escorted me away. I left submissively with them. In their limousine it occurred to me that we might be traveling for quite a distance.

"'There's a room registered for me in the hotel. I have to pay the bill beforehand,' I said.

"'Don't worry, it will be paid!'

"'Yes, but my suitcase is there with my things . . .'

"'The suitcase won't go anywhere!'

"I began to suspect that I had fallen under the protection of some important person. The officers did not explain where they were taking me, and I could sense tension and secretiveness in their behavior. I don't think that they themselves knew which magnate wanted to see me.

"Finally, we arrived at a hotel where a deluxe suite had been reserved for us. The hotel was located in central Moscow and my deluxe suite was the equal of any in Europe. The people gathered in the hotel lobby were clearly from the privileged class, but I did not know whether to rejoice or be apprehensive about my situation.

"It turned out that the hotel was, for some reason, inappropriate for our clandestine meeting, and within an hour we continued on. My companions and the chauffeur maintained total silence; I did not bother them with questions. I surmised they had orders to keep our final destination secret. Our second stop was in a cozy, unpopulated outskirt of the capital. Two high-ranking officers, probably colonels, stood on the porch of an ancient mansion along with three men in civilian clothes. This retinue accompanied me to the second floor, while I feverishly tried to imagine what this affair was all about. They led me into a spacious, luxuriantly furnished living room and left me alone. I remained there for half an hour.

"In walked a man whose appearance was so imposing that I fidgeted anxiously in my chair. He was dressed in civilian clothes, and had red cheeks and a fat nose. Only several years later did I discover through newspaper photographs that this person was Alexander Poskrebychev, the all-powerful assistant and personal secretary to Joseph Stalin. He asked me coldly, 'Are you carrying any weapons?' I was stupefied. Weapons? I never carried so much as a penknife! But my sense of humor did not desert me, and I bravely answered, tapping my finger significantly on my forehead, 'This is the only arsenal in which I store my weapons.' Without reacting to my quip, he frisked me quickly and professionally.

"The door opened softly a few minutes later; there appeared the familiar figure of the world-renowned dictator himself.

I immediately understood the mystery surrounding our trip. I also understood the question about weapons.

"Stalin greeted me softly but did not extend his hand. I answered politely, but then the devil took hold of me, and I said, 'I carried you in my arms just recently.' I expected him to be dumbfounded, but he possessed enviable self-restraint and only screwed up his eyes cunningly.

"'What do you mean, in your arms?' I explained that I had carried his huge portrait during a demonstration.

"'It seems you're a humorist as well,' he said with a strong Georgian accent. But I felt in his tone neither a capricious insult nor a sinister threat. He began to ask me several questions, all of a political nature. Never during that conversation did he inquire about my telepathic abilities. He questioned me about the situation in Poland, and about my meeting with Pilsudski and other Polish leaders.* Poland, at that time, was a thorn in his side.

"I was summoned to other meetings with Stalin. After the second one, he gave the KGB a detailed order to check my abilities. This took place somewhat later in Moscow. I believe that the experiment was proposed at his personal instigation.

"In the summer of 1940, I was asked to withdraw 100,000 rubles from a certain prominent branch of the state bank. I gave the bank teller a blank sheet of paper and mentally suggested that I was giving him a bona fide financial document. The crux of the experiment lay in the sheer enormity of the sum, because the teller would only be able to issue the funds after thoroughly checking the 'document.' He would have to be extremely careful with such a transaction. The teller, a rather short, middle-aged man with a thin gray moustache, took the paper, which was a sheet torn from an ordinary school notebook. He studied it

---

* Josef Pilsudski (1867–1935), Poland's premier and Minister of Military Affairs from 1926–1935, organized several campaigns against the Soviet Union. Stalin considered him an important enemy.

intently and for a long time, shifting his eyes between me and the document. He finally opened the safe and began to count out the money. This was essentially a repetition of that episode in Berlin where, by mental suggestion, I turned a scrap of paper into a railroad ticket.

"Three official witnesses, dressed in civilian clothes, had been placed at an inconspicuous distance. They immediately signed a document testifying to the experiment's success, and even counted the money I placed in the briefcase: it was all there.

"I returned once more to the cashier's window and handed him the same piece of paper, but this time I mentally commanded him to view the paper as it actually was. The only thing on the otherwise blank sheet was a stamp and his own signature. He cast a crazed glance at the paper, looked back at me in horror, then collapsed in his chair. He'd had a coronary! An ambulance was summoned immediately. Fortunately he recovered, but that incident still nags at my conscience.

"Another experiment consisted of my walking past three sets of security guards at a certain militarized establishment. The guards had been forewarned not to let me pass. Four guards were given a detailed description of me and the time of my anticipated exit, which was timed to a fraction of a minute. Yet I carried out the task quite easily.

"Although these experiments were carried out under the orders of Russia's highest ranking government officials, rumors about them soon trickled down to the general public, where they were exaggerated way out of proportion. One spiteful rumor was my supposed cooperation with the NKVD.* My political enemies and Moscow's scandalmongers perpetually promoted such stories.

"It was also alleged that I took part in the interrogations of prominent political prisoners in the cells of notorious Lubyanka prison, operated by the secret police. I also allegedly used

---

* People's Commissariat for Internal Affairs. — *editor's note.*

clairvoyance to examine the intentions of Stalin's closest aides, if he suspected them of opposition or conspiracy.

"As a medic, Tanya, you are familiar with the Hippocratic Oath physicians take at the beginning of their practice. They vow to use their medical skills only for the common good and their patients' welfare. So, when I first became conscious of my mysterious gift to telepathically influence people, I vowed I would never use it to hurt society or mankind. Not once have I broken this moral pledge, despite the slanders I've had to face.

"I should mention that the authorities themselves did not completely trust me at first. For quite a long time, they continued to thoroughly examine me; they have always been suspicious of any occult practice not fitting into their rigid materialistic framework. "Another reason, purely political, for their distrust of me was my background in Poland — a country with which Russia has always had hostile relations. During my first meeting with Stalin, I told him straight out that his country had no reliable western border, and that his very best friend, Hitler, would become his most vehement enemy. Stalin did not heed my warnings. I tried again and again to warn the authorities of Germany's imminent attack, but always received the reply that I would be notified when my advice was needed.

"Everything must end sometime. The suspicions subsided and I was able to work in relative freedom. I appeared before my first large Soviet audiences during tours in Odessa and Kharkov in the Ukraine, and then in Tbilisi, where I first received the news of Germany's attack on Russia.

"I remember that Sunday morning, June 22, 1941, down to the last detail. And I remember my own state of mind even better. I could not help but share in everyone's alarm, but I was further distressed by the gloomy thought that my previous warnings had been ignored. I could not personally participate in battle, or even give some kind of indirect help to the front. No matter what kind of patriot I showed myself to be, I would have been brushed aside because of the poor circulation in my legs. And who needed my psychological experiments at such an hour, I thought despondently.

"I returned to Moscow enshrouded in these gloomy thoughts. Our passenger train stopped at all the stations, sometimes for long periods of time. During every stop I walked about the platform, but I never attempted to penetrate the thoughts of the anxious people storming the ticket offices. I knew their thoughts were all the same: to escape the war's approaching holocaust.

"During these stops I found myself confronted with some unpleasant situations; I was detained several times by military patrols. My extravagant appearance and foreign accent invariably aroused suspicion. Radio broadcasts and hastily printed placards constantly reminded us the fascists had infiltrated the rear lines. Secret agents were everywhere.

"Even after my arrival in Moscow, I was arrested and spent several hours in a military command post while my identity was checked. In order to disguise my poor Russian, I tried to avoid conversation unless absolutely necessary. But I was not left to the mercy of fate. I learned that we were to be evacuated. My road led once more to the east, to western Siberia and the city of Novosibirsk.

"Even though I was far away, I unexpectedly participated in the war effort by performing for military units about to be sent to the front and in factory shops, where my spectators sat on boxes filled with ammunition, not theater seats. I was proud that, even in these hard times, I didn't retire from the stage. People still needed me.

"The Russian soul is an enigmatic one. It can both lift a person up and crush him, leaving him crying and laughing at the same time. The audience of soldiers couldn't help but know that many of them would never return from battle, but during my performances a feeling of healthy optimism prevailed. Virtually every other request asked me to perform some sort of humorous task.

"I won't try to hide the fact that I was paid for my performances like any gifted artist, and had considerable monetary resources. My expenses were small because I lived frugally and had no family. I had more than enough money for my needs. Now, I've never met a person who complained of having too much money, but in my situation, I thought it most reasonable to give my savings to the army. Such donations were then widely publicized to inspire Soviet patriotism. I decided that the best use for my money would be to buy a plane.

"I approached the government with my wish, and received in reply a telegram signed by Stalin himself. I read: 'To Comrade Wolf Messing: Accept my greetings and the gratitude of the Red Army, Comrade Wolf Messing, for your concern toward the air forces of the Red Army. Your wish will be carried out. J. Stalin.'

"I presented the first fighter plane to the military in 1942, and, two years later, gave the air force an even more sophisticated fighter. Some time I'll show you a copy of the newspaper, *The Baltic Flyer* (which had a large circulation during those years), in which appeared a long article written by war hero and aviator Captain Konstantin Kovalev telling of his meeting with me. It was a memorable meeting for me as well! I always laugh when I think of the trouble I had composing the dedicatory text for the plane's fuselage. They couldn't very well inscribe the ungrammatical text I composed! So they corrected it and painted the following inscription: 'A gift from Professor W. G. Messing to Baltic pilot and hero of the Soviet Union K. Kovalev. For victory over fascism!'

"That same year I spent considerable time touring Tashkent, where I formed a pleasant acquaintanceship with Aleksei Tolstoy, or, as he was called behind his back, the Red Count. Before this meeting, I had known Tolstoy only through his books and plays. After meeting him, and when my Russian improved, I immediately read his book *Walk in Torment*. I felt close to that book, for, since my childhood, I too walked more than once along life's thorny paths. I felt a kinship with the hero's rebellious spirit.

"During the war Moscow remained the epicenter of governmental life, but society's cultural and scientific elite soon evacuated the city and settled in the countryside. The cream of the intelligentsia gathered in especially large numbers in Tashkent. When I arrived at Tolstoy's residence, the writer Kornei I. Chukovsky, the widow of Maxim Gorki, the famous actor Ivan N. Bersenev, and some unfamiliar musicians were already sitting over tea. Tolstoy's apartment was a meeting place for the elite, and there I performed an improvised session for the guests, by finding Tolstoy's missing watch and describing a cross that his wife was wearing underneath her dress. Word of my arrival soon spread outside this close-knit little circle, and within three days my audience consisted of workers brought in from a Voronezh construction plant.

"All through the war I appeared before audiences that, although unsophisticated, received me warmly. I never concerned myself with the intellectual level of the audience. It was more important to me to leave audiences without any suspicion that I was either a shaman or a charlatan.

"In 1944, after an appearance in Novosibirsk, a young woman approached me backstage. She was a little overweight and sported a short hairdo. She wore a dark dress with a flower on her breast. Her voice was soft and pleasant, and she didn't mince words.

"'I think the introductory remarks that precede your entrance on the stage should be given in a different way,' she said.

"I was intrigued by her frankness. 'Well all right then,' I said, 'you try, if you think you're capable. My next show is in two days. Will that give you enough time to prepare?'

"'I think so,' the stranger replied.

"I met with her once more on the eve of my performance. I liked the manner in which she presented my introduction. She was concise and restrained, and obviously a very cultured person.

"'Do you have a long dress for the performance? Something like a ball gown?' I said. I thought that if she were interested in working with me, she'd agree to everything I suggested. But her answer was proud and independent.

"'I have nothing of that sort, but I'm sure that it's not necessary for your psychological experiments. Such a program falls outside the usual stage theatrics, so a tailored dark suit would be more suitable. I have such an outfit.'

"Such was my first meeting with the woman who later became my wife, friend, and assistant. You saw our relationship for yourself, Tanya."

Wolf Messing grew suddenly quiet, as if searching for some thread by which to continue his story. I understood that his soul was momentarily with his late wife. It was a touching moment, and I turned away my gaze instinctively. Messing mused for a moment and continued.

"In the first years following the war, I made the acquaintance of yet another remarkable person. I remember him with the greatest respect. I'm talking about the writer Aleksei Ignatiev, who wrote the dramatic epic *Fifty Years in the Ranks*. I don't think there is any need to discuss his book with you, Tanya. Right now it's not his work that I want to describe — I'm not a great expert on Russian literature but the unforgettable days of warmth and comfort he gave me. Please understand that for a wanderer like me, especially memorable are the days of … I know you're going to laugh to yourself … how can I say it … well … of perfect contentment."

Wolf fumbled for words.

"Ignatiev lived a full and complex life, and I felt so close to him because his wanderings reminded me of my own, although my first years could never be compared with his worldly travels. After all, he was a diplomat; he never had to travel about the world hidden beneath a coach seat! Later, however, when he was a political exile, he had occasion to taste the bitter fruit of a foreign land. When he returned to Moscow he lived on Staraya Square, and his doors were always open in the great tradition of Russian hospitality. I will always remember with pleasure the day he invited my wife and me to dinner. That meal was prepared with the touch of perfect aristocratic etiquette. The table, sparkling with silver, looked like a still life, from the little forks for the lemon slices to the Chinese-style sauce dish with the dragon's head on its handle. We drank tea from the finest Kuznetsov china. Granted, we had no need of all that silver; the only dish served that evening was buckwheat groats with crackling. But I can say with complete confidence that the most picky gourmet would have given that buckwheat its due. I've never tasted anything like it since! When I mention the spirit of Russian hospitality, I refer to the warm and generous atmosphere that anyone would find when visiting the Ignatiev family, whether in good times or bad.

"Ignatiev was also a brilliant conversationalist who knew both how to listen and how to tell a good story. Among the many personally autographed books with which I have been presented, I cherish his the most. Every time I read through my favorite passages, it's as if I am once more hearing the voice of Aleksei himself.

"All through the postwar years I traveled extensively around the country performing my psychological experiments. These tours enabled me to become better acquainted with this enormous country and its people. Making new friends was most important to me. I also had jealous enemies, of course, but my friends outnumbered them by far.

"Nor can I complain of any lack of public attention; I can't recall a single performance that wasn't sold out. The press, too, was excited about my work. Enthusiastic notices and articles appeared in the newspapers and in several scientific publications.

I always like to stress that my abilities could be discovered to some extent in every person. It is important for me to emphasize that there is nothing supernatural about my powers: they originate within the mind.

"The only group of spectators to ever greet me with reserve — to put it mildly — were the scientists. It wasn›t that they were against telepathic experiments. In fact they took an active part, both as spectators and panel members, in my performances. But they approached the boundaries of science with apprehension or, more properly, with caution. They wanted to fit my powers into some kind of explanatory framework.

"In 1950 my immediate bosses, the theatrical department of the Ministry of Culture, asked the Institute of Philosophy of the Academy of Sciences of the USSR to help prepare a text explaining the hard scientific basis of my powers. This request really wasn't surprising. Russia was going through a difficult period in the development of its philosophic thought, and Stalin had the last say both in philosophy and in science. If Stalin could not give an intelligent explanation of a scientific matter, then nobody from the lower scientific circles dared suggest one. Everything that was incomprehensible, unexplainable, or unacceptable to Stalin's materialism was banned, and I was told not to perform any feats incompatible with his ideology."

So it was that on May 17, 1950, Messing's directors received a notice from the Institute of Philosophy, Bureau of Tourism of the Committee of Artistic Affairs of the Council of Ministers of the USSR. This notice included a specifically prepared introductory text to be read at each performance. It was written by psychologist M.G. Yoroshevsky and approved by the psychological section of the Institute of Philosophy.

This carefully contrived text enabled the agency that booked Wolf's appearances throughout the Soviet Union to balance two vastly different elements within Soviet society. On the one hand, Russian tradition, filled with ancient folk practices and beliefs that revere the supernatural, ranges from as long ago as pre-Christian times, to as far away as the shamanistic practices of eastern Siberia. On the other hand, Marxist materialism denies all "idealism" or mystical phenomena. Soviet scientists studying parapsychological phenomena and, before that, spiritual practices, carefully avoided public attention during Stalin's lifetime. His personal fascination with Messing was the exception that proved the rule, and the rule in the mid-1920s made psychic research and parapsychology taboo. These fields remained underground until after Stalin's death in 1953.

Credit for the eventual acceptance of parapsychological studies as a legitimate scientific undertaking must largely go to Leonid L. Vasiliev, to whom I have referred several times. During the Nikita Khrushchev decade of cultural and scientific "thaw," parapsychology experienced a relative boom. While Wolf Messing was never personally examined in Soviet psychophysiological laboratories, experiments clearly inspired by his performances were undertaken from the mid-1950s onward. Messing himself was, historically speaking, a descendant of a generation of Polish psychics prominent in the late nineteenth and early twentieth centuries. There was a strong link between Polish psychic investigators and those in France, notably the group formed by the Institut Metapsychique International, with whom Dr. Vasiliev remained in constant, though at times clandestine, contact.

Vasiliev used a sensational report concerning an alleged United States navy experiment in long distance telepathy between a nuclear submarine and a naval base to create public support for official Soviet studies of parapsychology. This report, published in early 1960 in the Parisian magazine *Science et Vie*, was later discredited, but it certainly aroused official interest in Leningrad and Moscow. Vasiliev was also able to establish an ideological bridge between public fascination with parapsychological phenomena and Marxist materialism. In his writings he stated, in effect, that it was appropriate to test claims for abilities such as telepathy by strictly physiological means, and to thus make a definitive decision on the legitimacy of such claims.

As I have noted, public rumors were rampant about Messing's use by the KGB, the secret police, and its predecessor agencies. Wolf apparently managed to escape all KGB requests to use or even simply test his skills. For this purpose it was quite convenient for him to present himself, as did the state theatrical management, as a simple stage performer. It is fair to say, I think, that he remained an enigma to the KGB, just as he did to the scientific establishment.

By the time of his death, Krushchev's fall and the "thaw" period had long passed, and parapsychology had once again entered a twilight zone. Particularly ominous was that the KGB, as well as the military, had begun to take parapsychology very seriously and were, in fact, competing with the Soviet Academy of Science as to how, and by whom, parapsychological phenomena were to be studied. In September, 1973, the Moscow journal *Questions of Philosophy* published an article coauthored by four prominent psychologists entitled "Parapsychology: Fiction or Reality?" The authors maintain that the study of this field is too critical and complex to be left in the hands of self-styled parapsychologists, but should instead be undertaken by professional psychologists so that "the attention of serious scientific organizations" might be properly directed toward "unanswered questions of the human psyche."

The plea for control over parapsychological research by the Soviet psychological establishment did not, however, lead to the authors' desired results. KGB and military interest in the field had, by then, become too strong to permit such delicate studies of "the human psyche" to slip into purely academic hands. The subsequent developments would have been highly distasteful to Wolf Messing. Only one example of this trend needs to be cited. In 1965, the bionics section of the A. S. Popov Scientific-Technical Society for Radio Engineering, Electronics and Communications in Moscow began studies in telepathy, although it labeled the field "biological communication." Under its aegis, the Laboratory for Bio-Information was created, and it functioned for several years by experimenting in precisely the areas in which Messing had so long excelled. However, after Khrushchev's fall, and following the emergence of Yuri Andropov (later General Secretary of the Soviet Communist

Party) as head of the KGB in 1967, control over parapsychological studies was severely tightened, and experiments in this field were categorized as "secret." Even the Laboratory for Bio-Information came under scrutiny, and several of its members were ousted for having shown themselves too "idealistic." The charge was actually that the experimenters had proved too squeamish when dealing with the delicate psyches of their human experimental subjects. The unit was quietly reorganized as the Laboratory for Bio-Electronics, but its work, previously publicized at least in part, was now kept in utmost secrecy.

8

Soviet Science "Explains" Telepathy

For the rest of the years I remained friends with Messing, I tried to find a viable explanation for telepathy. The press made some attempts, but they were usually attacked by the scientific establishment as soon as they were proposed. Belief in the very existence of telepathy was attacked for being antimaterialistic, pseudoscientific, and a bourgeoise superstition.

The most prominent and vocal debunker was Professor Alexander Kitaygorodsky. He and his fellow skeptics were unable to come up with serious explanations for the sixth sense or parapsychological phenomena in general. They set out to explain to the public that Messing's powers could be accounted for via pure rationality, and they drew upon the work of Ivan Pavlov — the great Russian physiologist — for their inspiration. They even proposed a theory for Wolf Messing's abilities based on his research. Every evening before Messing's entrance onto the stage, Aida had to read the text composed by Yaroshevsky, to whom I referred in the previous chapter. I don't know whether this explanation ever convinced the audience, but I would like to reproduce it here. The original text, which is extremely repetitious and circumlocuted, is edited for this book.

The psychological experiments you are about to witness testify to the fact that Wolf Messing possesses some extraordinary powers. He is capable of carrying out any command — precisely and unerringly — that anyone present may wish to mentally dictate to him. At first glance, this capability may seem to be the result of some supernatural power. However, there is nothing supernatural in the performance.

These demonstrations can be completely explained according to the canons of conventional hard science. In order to make the nature of these demonstrations clear to you, I will briefly explain the basis of his gift.

The brain represents the mental organ within man. The precise mechanisms by which it functions have been explained by the Russian scientists I. M. Sechenov and I. P. Pavlov. By the end of the last century, Sechenov had already outlined the basis of the brain's reflex activity, and Pavlov later expanded his theories. Pavlov demonstrated that all mental processes and sensations — feelings, concepts, thoughts — represent the output of the brain's neurons.

Reflecting input derived from the outside world, the brain regulates all the physiological processes that give rise to biological lift. When a person thinks about something, his brain cells instantly transmit impulses to the rest of his body. For example, if a person thinks of taking some object into his hand, the brain will translate this thought into an impulse that manipulates the hand muscles. This impulse is small, but it definitely exists. You can prove it for yourself by conducting a simple experiment. Take a string and attach a weight to it, so that you have a makeshift pendulum. Then, begin to think about some sort of movement — for example, think of the pendulum rotating clockwise. The more intensely you concentrate, the more clearly the weight will begin to rotate in the manner you are thinking of. This phenomenon can be easily explained: that part of the brain underlying human thought is directly connected with that part regulating our motor functions. Simply speaking, thought is connected to motion. A bicyclist needs only to vividly imagine that he is in danger of running into a pile of rocks, and he will involuntarily make the exact motions that will fulfill his fears. While crossing a narrow plank, you need only to imagine that you are in danger of falling, and your equilibrium will be upset. In each instance, your thoughts have involuntarily influenced your physical behavior. Scientists call these examples "ideomotor" acts.

The research of those following the leads of Pavlov, K. M. Bykov, and others has outlined the process in some detail. Not only can thoughts produce involuntary muscular impulses, but also changes in blood circulation, the central nervous system's excitability, and so forth.

Recently, sensitive instruments were employed to register the precise currents that excite muscles when they are influenced by a specific thought. It was discovered that if a person closes his eyes and thinks of some tall object — a tower, for example — his eyeballs will appear as though he were really looking upward.

If electrodes were placed on a person's tongue and larynx and then connected to a sufficiently sensitive galvanometer, the readings would register weak impulses, as if he spoke his thoughts. These scientific experiments prove that the body can respond to weak messages from the brain, and that these impulses can be detected.

All perception arises from our five sensory organs. Now, in order for a sensation to register in the brain, that sensation must first reach a certain magnitude. For example, you do not usually notice your watch ticking, but if you bring it close enough to your ear, the ticking will become clear. The sensory organs vary in their acuity from person to person, and some people possess a phenomenally high level of sensitivity.

Many of you know of the heightened sensitivity of the blind and deaf. Because they cannot use their sight or hearing, their other sense perceptions become keener. Walking along a familiar street, they know which house they are passing by its smell, or detect an approaching person or car by weak vibrations. These perceptual abilities can also be enhanced deliberately through training. What you will witness today is completely explanable by these precepts...

And with a pregnant pause, Aida would end her introduction. To what extent is this explanation true? To what extent was the speech a theatrical device to excite the audience's curiosity even further? I don't think the process behind Messing's powers was clear even to Aida herself, though she witnessed the experiments almost daily for twenty years.

It is unfortunate that the peak of Messing's career was during Stalin's repressive dictatorship. After Stalin's death science recovered and such fields as cybernetics came into their own. Had Messing's creative work come to light two decades later, who knows what discoveries could have been made. His abilities would at least have been respected, and serious research designed to investigate them. But the difficult Stalin years never allowed Wolf this respect, and Russia's greatest psychic was reduced to giving theatrical performances to earn his living.

Does genuine telepathy really exist? The electromagnetic spectrum has been well studied, and no field effect exists that could explain such a phenomenon. Perhaps there does exist in nature an as yet unknown semiphysical field that can't be recorded by science's present instruments. When the electromagnetic field was discovered by Heinrich Hertz in 1886, no one could have imagined the transmission of sounds and images we take for granted today. Perhaps in the future someone will discover a way to explain what we call telepathy. I don't think any scientist, or Wolf Messing himself, could consciously explain his rare gifts. They represent mysteries that elude our present scientific methods. It was probably easier and simpler for Soviet scientists in the 1940s and 1950s to offer purely rational explanations for Wolf's sixth sense than to grapple with the real secrets housed within his brain.

Let's take a look at evidence, derived from science and popular culture, directly pointing to the existence of supernormal faculties in man.

The direct transmission of thought is a possibility mankind has contemplated through the ages. The idea no doubt first arose centuries ago, inspired by common, everyday experiences. We know that people often have premonitions or presentiments when something terrible is about to happen to their family or friends, even if they are miles away from them. Many examples could be cited. During World War II, for example, many stories were told of mothers and wives who knew immediately when their sons or husbands were killed at the front. Even the skeptic could hardly attribute such events to coincidence, i.e., that it's more likely that a person will be killed in a large scale war than survive. Such an objection would be cogent, except that these people invariably "received" their impressions at the precise day and hour of death.

The following story is told by Hans Berger, still remembered for his discovery of electroencephalography, in his pamphlet *Psyche*. As far as I am aware, this is the first time it has been translated into English.

The following happened when — as a nineteen-year-old student — I barely escaped certain death during some military exercises in Wurzburg. I was escorting artillery weapons in a wagon pulled by six horses. My horse stumbled while crossing the edge of a steep mountain road and I almost fell beneath the wheels of the cart. Luckily the horses were stopped in time and I was saved. I was unhurt but badly frightened. The incident took place on the morning of a lovely spring day, but that very evening I received a telegram from my father asking whether I was all right. That was the first and only time in my life that I ever received such an inquiry from him.

It turned out that my eldest sister, with whom I was especially close, insisted that the telegram be sent. She somehow "knew" that an accident had befallen me. Since at that time my parents were living in Koburg, the incident was a clear example of the spontaneous transmission of thought. At a time of grave danger, I acted as some sort of transmitter and my sister became the receiver.

Hans Berger also cites this example:

One morning while I was getting dressed I suddenly had a strange sensation. I was as if I were with an old school friend I hadn't seen for twenty years. While on my way to work at the clinic, this thought kept returning and I couldn't get rid of it. Four hours later, the director of the clinic told me that a certain gentleman wished to talk to me about an important matter. That gentleman turned out to be my friend.

A similar story is told by Leonid Vasiliev in his book *Mental Suggestion at a Distance*. When the scientist was twelve years old, he spent the summer at his aunt's country home not far from the city of Pskov. His parents had gone to the Czechoslovakian spa of Karlsbad to take a water cure. One day toward evening,

Leonid and his brother and sister decided to climb a willow tree that hung over a river bank. Leonid fell from the tree and into the river. He couldn't swim and was in imminent danger of drowning. Luckily, he was able to grab hold of a low branch and make his way up the river bank, while his brother and sister watched in horror. The children were afraid that they'd be punished; they were soaked to the skin and Leonid lost his school cap. They knew their aunt would be angry.

When she heard the story, however, she promised not to write to their parents about the incident. They were naturally amazed when their mother, upon her return, recounted the incident in full detail, mentioning the cap, the willow tree, and so forth. She had seen it all in a dream so vivid that she urged her husband to send a telegram to Pskov. Leonid's father confessed that he never sent the telegram; he went to the telegraph office only to calm his wife, and instead took a nap there!

Even if we place our faith in science, doesn't the existence of such phenomena contradict a purely material view of the world? Doesn't it point to some unknown field existing around us? Gaps exist in our knowledge of nature. Serious scientists continue to search for some physical process explaining telepathy, but perhaps there is no such physical basis.

The brain clearly harbors several mysteries. The secrets of hypnosis, for example, were well known to the priests of ancient Egypt and Babylon. The oracles of ancient Greece were purported experts in making predictions. In our own day, the power of the mind to control the body are well-known, too. Some fascinating experiments conducted by the University of London Council for Psychical Investigations with Kuda Bux, a fakir from India,[*] demonstrate the power of the mind to control the body. The fakir walked across a pit filled with red-hot coals and embers having a surface temperature of four hundred degrees centigrade. The

---

[*] See Harry Price, "A Report on Two Experimental Fire-Walks." In *Bulletin II*, University of London Council for Psychical Investigation, 1936.

soles of his feet (examined before the experiment to make sure they were not chemically coated) showed no trace of burning. But the most amazing and mysterious part was yet to come. Bux, about to repeat his walk a second time, suddenly refused to continue.

"Something broke in me," he explained. "forgive me, but I cannot repeat the experiment. I have lost faith in myself and might burn myself badly."

This is a most revealing statement. It appears that the fakir's state of mind played a significant role in his fire-walking. This fact shouldn't strike anyone as absurd; the mind controls the body in a unique way. A hypnotist can produce burn marks in a subject's body through pure suggestion; similar autosuggestion is undoubtedly the key to most cases of stigmata. Many devout Christians throughout history have borne the marks of the crucifixion on their bodies, and sometimes these wounds have even bled. No doubt in the future, psychologists will discover exactly how this phenomenon takes place, but it is clear that the explanation will be found within the brain.

No wonder of the physical world can compare with the secrets of the brain. It is the source of our highest creative endeavors, which have filled the world with gifts such as art and science. It is amazing that the brain still remains such a mystery. It represents an unknown world whose language we are just beginning to understand.

9

Occultism's Dark Side

The ancient Greek sophist Gorgius of Lentini, who was famous for his powers of oratory, said that the word is a great master. It can accomplish miraculous deeds: it can banish fear and sadness, and inspire compassion.

I once sat with Wolf as he recited a passage from a poem dedicated to him by Robert Rozhdestvensky. He stopped to reach for his accursed cigarettes, while I thought back to my own first attempt at writing poetry at the time I was tearing back and forth between my two passions — medicine and journalism. A poem I once wrote about building a bridge of goodwill to unite one heart with another, now seemed more appropriate than ever. What a great gift it must be to transfer your thoughts to another person, I thought. This ability had been given to someone — Wolf — capable of building bridges between human hearts only in the name of truth and beauty. Wolf almost seemed to hear my secret thoughts as he continued his life's story.

"You see, Robert Rozhdestvensky speaks in his poem as if I literally *read* other people's thoughts," he began, "but is that actually the way I do it? More accurately, I *perceive* the thoughts of other people. More often than not, I perceive these impressions as abstractions and images that merely signify actions or places.

"My friend, the writer and journalist Mikhail Vasiliev, with whom I spent several days at his country house near Moscow, asked me a thousand times how my powers worked. I knew his interest wasn't sparked by the curiosity of a school boy asking the secret of a card trick. Vasiliev was then collecting material for a series of books to be called *Man and the Universe*. How could I answer him? How is it done? I don't want to surround myself with mystery, nor elevate myself up among the gods. In any event, I do not consider my talent to be any more extraordinary than the talents of others. After all, we encounter so many gifted people at every turn! I'll give an example of the difficulty of explaining my abilities.

"Imagine that you have found yourself in a country of the blind, the land that H. G. Wells described in his famous story. The people living in this country don't even suspect the existence of such a power as sight, and you are the only sighted person there. A meticulous inquirer is trying to figure out how you can 'know' about objects that are ten, hundreds, or even thousands of yards away. Could you really explain the images you see to him? This is my situation when I am asked about my gifts. You would be in a better position to explain physical sight: you could explain how light waves function, how such waves reflect into the eye's lens, and so forth. A physical process explains sight. You have the findings of a cohort of scientists to work with. But, in explaining my powers, it is impossible to even begin."

For a long time, I had wanted to ask Messing about his encounters with other telepaths, and what he thought of their capabilities. He was about to broach the topic himself and he grew visibly excited when I asked.

"Of course I've met them, Taibele," he began. "I have never considered myself unique. You can only have exclusive rights to an invention, and I never invented the sixth sense. I inherited my abilities, though I don't know from whom.

"I can recall several meetings with telepaths from other countries, and I've also seen more than a few blatant charlatans. These latter were coarse scoundrels who led the public by the nose by means of the most puerile tricks. Most people have seen the type of performance these charlatans give. As a rule, two people come out on stage, usually a man and a woman working in collaboration. The eyes of the first are tightly bound with a black cloth, and someone from the audience is invited on stage to verify that the cloth is tightly tied and impossible to see through. This of course implies that any conscious deception has been excluded. Then the assistant steps into the auditorium to begin the act. She stops near, let's say, a military officer in full dress uniform with four rows of ribbons and the gold star of a war hero on his jacket. The assistant then engages in the following conversation with the 'telepath'."

"Who is next to me?"

"A soldier."

"Think. Define him more clearly!"

"Colonel, infantry."

"More precisely?"

"Infantry guard."

"What am I touching?"

"Military decorations."

"More exactly?"

"A ribbon signifying the Order of the Red Banner."

"How many orders does he have in all? Don't answer immediately… count."

"Four."

"Correct. And who am I standing beside now?"

Such a dialogue could be carried on indefinitely. I've observed these and similar sessions with mixed feelings. Simply from my vantage point as a spectator, I would give the performer his due. He has obviously trained well, and he entertains me just like a magician would. But that's where my admiration would end, since these performers don't have the decency to present themselves as clever tricksters. The well-known illusionists Dick Chitashvili, Yefim, and Polina Kubansky could snatch ten lighted cigarettes out of thin air right before your eyes, but they never claimed to really 'materialize' them. They were skilled magicians and performed as magicians. But the telepathic performance I've just described is a deliberate deception threatening to undermine public respect for parapsychology.

"Let's look at this performance again. Obviously the 'psychic' delivered information from an easily decipherable spoken code. The couple prearranged that the assistant would approach a soldier, and the rest was easy. When the assistant asks him to think *more clearly*, that's a cue to the performer that the soldier is a colonel with the infantry; *more precisely* signifies a guard; *touching* signifies military decorations; and *more exactly* signifies the Order of the Red Banner. When she asks how many orders the soldier has, she says *Don't answer immediately, count*, a phrase consisting of *four* words.

"This simple code is the secret of the show. If, instead of saying *think, define more clearly*, the assistant had said only *define more clearly*, she would designate a lieutenant colonel. If she had said only *think*, she would designate a general. If, instead of saying *what am I touching*, the accomplice said *what do I have my hand on*, she would perhaps signify a shoulder strap, not military decorations."

"The possibilities of transmitting information by these and similar codes are infinite, and anybody with a good memory can learn to master them."

Wolf was obviously insulted by such performances, and, after describing other, similar forms of fakery, he dropped the subject.

"Aside from thought reading," he then continued, "I also possess the ability to place myself in a cataleptic state. Many of the great yogis have mastered this power, which I witnessed more than once in India. I developed this power early in childhood. Remember, this power made it possible for me to earn my living in Berlin, where I was billed as the living corpse.

"Catalepsy is a state of total immobility in which the extremities and muscles become phenomenally rigid. When I enter into such a state, you can place the back of my head on the seat of one chair and my heels on another to create a kind of bridge. While I'm in that position, even a rather large person can sit on me — a person I probably couldn't lift an inch off the ground under normal circumstances. But, while in the cataleptic state, I can support his weight easily and for an extended period of time. My pulse cannot be felt, my breathing ceases, and the beating of my heart is barely perceptible.

"Pavlov explained that such a state can be produced in some people through sudden shock, hysteria, or hypnosis. He believed it resulted when the brain's cerebral cortex switches off while the underlying branches of the neural-motor system remain active.

"I can enter into this state voluntarily, though only after a lengthy preparation. Sometimes it takes me several hours to mobilize my will. In recent years I've demonstrated this ability less and less, because I've been concentrating on my psychic performances. When I was much younger, though, catalepsy was an indispensible part of all my performances, especially during my European tours. But even in this field, I found tricksters demonstrating similar effects with the aid of all sorts of mechanical contrivances. Evidently, no sphere of human activity is free of fraud.

"Here in the West, occult science remains extremely popular and has numerous practitioners and disciples. I've seen the garishly painted little houses and shacks of fortunetellers, magicians, wizards, and chiromancers on the Champs d'Elysées in Paris, on the Unter den Linden in Berlin, and on the streets of Stockholm, Buenos Aires, Tokyo, and Casablanca.

"I can remember the legendary chiromancer Pifelo, a tall, thin man with long arms protruding from his sleeves, who handed out 'miracle-working' talismans to passersby — for a fee, of course. He was the first of his breed. He had miraculous knickknacks ready for every possible worldly need or problem. He could conjure up talismans to protect you from injury in battle, give you success in business, and reverse infertility in women. Poor Pifelo never became wealthy himself, however.

"I remember, too, the psychographologist Schiller-Shkolnik.

Not only could he determine a person's character by his handwriting, which is not all that complicated, but he could foretell the future and disclose the past.

"I support the view that a person's handwriting expresses his personality. Cogent comments on the subject were made by Sigmund Freud, who found meaning in our everyday slips of the tongue or pen, and in our predilection to repeat certain words.* The great German poet, dramatist, and novelist Johann Wolfgang von Goethe, who had an extensive collection of autographs, was also convinced that a person's character and spiritual makeup were revealed by his calligraphy. Whether we can predict a person's past or future from his handwriting is, however, a subject I approach with the most profound skepticism.

"I can't help but recall the world of spiritualism, with its psychic mediums, table-turning seances, and secret societies. I'll have to confess that I once belonged to this otherworldly brotherhood and actively participated in their practices. During the 1930s, in fact, spiritualism was rather fashionable in certain Polish circles. Because of the sheer number of mediums available in the country, the ranks of the spiritualists swelled.

"The basis of spiritualist belief is that the souls of the dead can, under certain conditions, enter into communion with those of us still living. In order to bring about such contact, it is first necessary to procure the services of a medium — a psychic capable of communicating with the other world. The spiritualists in our group ordinarily gathered together with a medium. Skeptics were asked to leave, because it was felt that contact could be made only if all those present deeply believed in the possibility. It was thought that even one such person would somehow negatively influence conditions.

"The seances varied from session to session and from medium to medium; different psychics use different procedures. Some

---

* Sigmund Freud explains the meaning behind these slips in *The Psychopathology of Everyday Life* published in 1904, and in English in 1914.

of them employ simple table turning, while others use slate-writing — writings from the other side appearing suddenly on sealed chalk slates. Although they were few in number, some mediums could produce materializations. But the simplest method was communication through knockings. For these sessions, the medium entered into a trance similar to hypnosis and, after a short period of time, the spirits would knock on a door or wall announcing their presence. Those in attendance could then ask the most unpredictable questions, responded to by a long series of monotonous knocks. The number of raps in each series indicated a specific letter of the alphabet. Words and entire sentences could be formed from the raps, though sometimes the interpretations we gave them were severely strained!

"The most powerful medium in our group was thought to be a certain Jan Guzik.* He called forth the spirits of Napoleon, Alexander the Great, Adam Mickewicz, and even Christopher Columbus. I regret that I was never impudent enough to ask him to call forth the spirits of Adam or Eve, or both simultaneously, so I could hear their different views on the snake that tempted them. Later I came to consider spiritualism pure hokum and probably the result of mass hypnosis and suggestion. Once, while visiting London, I attended a circus performance in which magicians parodied all the spiritualist's experiments, exposing the clever stunts behind them."

The spiritualistic traditions of the nineteenth century, of which much of recent psychic research and parapsychology is heir, are certainly easily mimicked by skilled stage magicians. The parody Messing observed at the circus was perhaps most

---

* Jan Guzik (1875-1928) was thoroughly tested by several scientists. He gave a series of fifteen seances in Warsaw in September 1921 for Professor Gustave Geley, who reported them in his *Clairvoyance and Materialization.* Even though Geley was impressed by Guzik, other researchers considered him a complete fraud. An entirely negative report on his powers was issued by the Sorbonne in 1923. He was subsequently caught in fraud by flashlight photography in Krakow the following year. — *editor's note.*

proficiently performed by the world-renowned stage magician Harry Houdini. And yet, many spontaneous spiritistic phenomena remain unexplained and unduplicated by stage magic. And while Wolf's memories linked seances with Poland, there is also a deep and virtually ineradicable spiritistic tradition within Russia as well as other regions within the Soviet Union.

Perhaps one of the most startling contemporary public displays of this tradition emerged during the famous Twentieth Congress of the Communist Party of the Soviet Union in 1956, where Khrushchev gave his historic speech revealing the inhuman practices of the Stalin era and exposing the "cult of the personality" that had characterized a quarter century of Soviet history. At this congress a former student of Vladimir I. Lenin, founder of the Soviet state, stood up and passionately, exclaimed, in the presence of some five thousand delegates, that Lenin's disembodied presence told her he could no longer bear sharing his tomb with the body of Stalin. The former student, Darya Lazurkina, was by then a frail, elderly woman who had herself become one of Stalin's victims in 1937.

One published account of the congress noted that Lazurkina's invocation of Lenin, recalled her nineteen and one-half years in prisons, labor camps, and domestic exiles. But, she said, "I always had Lenin in my heart and asked him what to do." She added: "Yesterday I consulted Lenin again, and he seemed to stand before me as if alive and said, 'It is unpleasant for me to be next to Stalin, who caused the party so much harm.'" Whatever the direct impact of this testimony, which parapsychologists might categorize as a visually and orally perceived apparition, Stalin's body was subsequently removed from the Red Square mausoleum and reburied in a Kremlin cemetery.

Lazurkina's testimony should be viewed against the historical background of spiritualism in prerevolutionary Russia, which reflected nineteenth-century fascination with spiritistic phenomena, in Europe as well as the United States.

One internationally known medium, Daniel Dunglas Home, visited the royal court at St. Petersburg to much acclaim. Also, a journal devoted to spiritualistic and psychic phenomena was published in Russia's capital city from 1857 to 1867. Its very name, *Vestnik Evropy* (*European Messenger*), reflected the international character of psychic studies during that period.

Skeptics and critics were vocal even then. Among them was a pioneer in chemistry and physics, Dimitry I. Mendeleyev, who organized an investigating committee within St. Petersburg's Physical Society devoted to the exposure of fraudulent mediums. His most prominent antagonist was Alexander N. Aksakov, whose writings on spiritualistic and related phenomena were published in Germany, France, Great Britain, and the United States.

The Russian Society for Experimental Psychology was established in 1891, and its members examined the range of phenomena, including clairvoyance and telepathy, that Messing later displayed so dramatically. At the turn of the century, *Rebus*, a Russian journal devoted exclusively to spiritualism, was published in St. Petersburg. World War I and the Bolshevik Revolution brought an end to this trend, but the many deaths during both wars kept private interest in seance phenomena and life-after-death studies high.

Messing's own work brought him into contact with many occultists. He said he spent "so much time discussing" them "because I encountered them so often.

"I knew many of them closely, which is why I've discovered their techniques to dupe the public. I therefore found the honesty of the fakir Ben Ali, who worked at one time with the Warsaw Circus, refreshing. He was much like me in spirit and much more likeable than most performers. His best number was called 'the shot.' He was fired at with a pistol, and he invariably caught the bullets in flight with his bare hand. Spectators with weak nerves usually went into hysterics, but Ali always survived the ordeal. Once there was a skeptical officer among the spectators who offered to take a shot at Ben Ali with his own pistol. With bitter irony, Ali said: 'If you were in my place, dear sir, would you agree to be killed for some five zlotys a day!'

"The primary thing, from my point of view, is to differentiate occultism and charlatanry from the real existence of telepathy, which should be subject to rigid and serious scientific testing. It's a sad fact that there are more charlatans than genuine psychics today, and they have trivialized this still unresolved scientific mystery. They have inured society to be overly skeptical when the very subject is brought up. There exists more reason for this skepticism; some telepaths themselves are guilty of exaggerating their powers, and others have used their skills purely for mercenary reasons.

"Some evidence exists that the brilliant and famous international adventurer Count Cagliostro, who lived in the troubled eighteenth century, possessed significant telepathic abilities. Not without success, he often passed himself off as a physician of remarkable capabilities. He would also appear before his admiring contemporaries claiming to be a natural scientist, or a brilliant alchemist in possession of the Philosopher's Stone. He also duped his trusting cohorts in convincing them of his immortality, and claimed to be thousands of years old. But he was not successful when playing the role of clairvoyant.

"To the chagrin of his descendants, this brilliant rogue left behind no material evidence of his exceptional talents. Nor were his memoirs ever preserved in notes or diaries, though some clever forgeries have surfaced. This enigmatic figure sparked the imagination of many people, including such writers as Alexander Dumas and Tolstoy, who fashioned their literary representations of him from questionable legends.

"I too became interested in Cagliostro and once tried to analyze some of the testimony of his contemporaries. You have to give the devil his due: he was a first-class, talented scoundrel, and I have little doubt that telepathy was in his arsenal of effects. Cagliostro undoubtedly belonged in the category of psychics who exaggerate their powers and use their gifts for mercenary reasons. Erik Jan Hannussen should also be placed in this class.

"The controversy over telepathy still exists today, of course. I learned of an interesting and informal meeting between Karl Nikolaev, a young amateur telepath, and Alexander Kitaygorodsky, known for his skepticism to telepathy. Professor Kitaygorodsky had just published an article in the *Literary Gazette* on this intriguing topic. The article concluded that, since it is impossible to explain the transmission of thought, whether telepathy exists is a moot point. The statement was a blow to believers. Karl Nikolaev went to the editorial office of the magazine *Znanye-Sila (Knowledge is Strength)* and announced his desire to meet Kitaygorodsky. He asked that experiments be conducted with him under the supervision of several impartial observers. This was one young psychic's honest and direct approach to the controversy. Nikolaev tried to demonstrate everything he was capable of, and to some extent he succeeded in shaking the skepticism of the old and eminent scholar.

"Kitaygorodsky remarked that he could try to give his final evaluation of the experiment objectively and offered to write a second article recommending that telepathy should at least be seriously studied. In the end, however, Kitaygorodsky stuck to his original position. The article admitted that, in certain instances, the experiments with Nikolaev were successful and impressive, but he concluded Nikolaev was nothing more than an excellent guesser. Kitaygorodsky's evaluations and his conclusions are old-fashioned and conservative, and simply can't hold water.

"It has long been known that the electrical activity within the brain reflects our thought processes. New instruments, such as the electroencephalograph, now make it possible to record this activity. It's been discovered that the more intensely a person concentrates, the greater the amplitude and frequency of electrical impulses. Why can't this activity be the basis for telepathy? The usual objection to this theory is that brain's electrical output is too small to be perceptible from even a short distance. But I don't think this objection should be taken seriously, and it doesn't address the entire issue."

Messing was, of course, quite right; modern medical technology has provided parapsychology with a new and highly efficient set of tools. In fact, Karl Nikolaev and his telepathic partner, the biophysicist Yuri Kamensky, were repeatedly and carefully examined by the Laboratory for Bio-Information, then operating in Moscow under the direction of Professor Ippolite Kogan, noted for his research in radio engineering. In a series of thought transmission experiments between Moscow and Novosibirsk, and between other distant cities, the two men underwent a variety of tests ranging from transmitting codes through morse signals, to guessing a variety of household items "sent" to Nikolaev by his partner. Their brains and hearts were monitored during these tests, with elaborate protocols documenting their careful preparation and execution. It should not, however, be assumed that the results were uniformly positive, or that they were received without controversy. However, the increasingly serious attention paid to parapsychological phenomena by the Soviet scientific community was itself quite startling.

Wolf Messing did not use partners, nor did the various laboratories, to my knowledge, test his special skills under technologically controlled conditions. Psychic skills are as varied and elusive as other talents, and psychics who perform exceedingly well in spontaneous situations, or with the stimulus of audience participation, often do not function well in cold and impersonal laboratory settings.

Wolf recalled that Kitaygorodsky spoke of the phenomenon that has become known as "subliminal perception" and sought to use it to document the elusive subtlety of our sensory perceptions. Kitaygorodsky specifically mentioned experiments that, as he put it, "demonstrated the human eye was capable of responding to subliminal messages flashed before it. He explained:

"For example, a commercial advertisement lasting no more than $1/25^{th}$ of a second can be placed in the middle of a film. It won't be noticed by the viewer, but its message will infiltrate the viewer's consciousness. Why shouldn't the respected scientist entertain the notion that the brain might be similarly sensitive to electrochemical currents generated by another brain? Couldn't a tiny emission from an electromagnetic field set up some sort of resonance in another person's brain ?

"The second objection to the electromagnetic wave theory of telepathy is that these radiations represent an unimportant by-product of thought — something like smoke from a factory chimney. I readily agree with this point, but it seems to me that the smoke might reveal something important about what's being produced! The smoke from a factory burning mercury differs from that of a power station's boiler.

"Forgive me for being metaphorical, but isn't it possible that some people possess highly refined supersenses that can accurately interpret these various types of 'smoke,' precisely determining the process by which it is produced, and therefore *what* the factory is producing? Serious experiments must be conducted to determine whether the electromagnetic field carries telepathic transmissions.

"As for my telepathic skill, I can only say that it is of little concern to me whether or not I have physical contact with my inductor. It is of little significance whether I hold his wrist or he holds mine. It is much easier for most telepaths to penetrate another person's thoughts while holding his hand. Perhaps this fact will help scientists in their search to understand telepathy."

10

The Enigma
of Messing's Gifts

During its first century, the Institute of Diplomatic Relations produced a series of outstanding spokesmen. While engaged in negotiations, they have often staggered their rivals or allies with their extraordinary political knowledge and expertise. Undoubtedly, the information they brought to negotiating tables was supplied by the Soviet secret service network, but some diplomats also possessed the gift of reading the thoughts of their rivals. Of course, the diplomats were helped by their expert knowledge of human psychology, but sometimes they were aided by the sixth sense.

This is but a simple example of how some people use telepathy in their daily lives, sometimes without even realizing it. Similarly, I can recall a story Wolf liked to tell about a border guard who worked in customs. He was young and handsome, with dark hair and brown eyes, and his uniform fit so perfectly that it seemed to have been custom-made. He seemed to unknowingly use his psychic senses during work. His duty was to make sure the luggage crossing the border was "clean," i.e., without forged documents, gold, drugs, illicit gems, or other contraband. By merely casting a cursory glance at a traveler's baggage, he could easily spot their hiding places. If the contraband was hidden on the smuggler's body, the guard looked him in the eye and said something like, "Remove your left boot and unscrew the heel,"or "Does the double bottom of your traveling bag open from the inside or the outside?"

When asked *how* he always knew where to find these hidden items, he could never give a concrete answer. "I don't know; I sense it intuitively," he would say.

The guard was undoubtedly psychic, but he obviously didn't realize it, and were he to witness one of Messing's performances, he'd probably be just as astonished as everyone else. Searching for hidden objects was a significant part of most of Wolf Messing's performances.

To give you a better idea of Wolf's performances, I'd like to cite some newspaper and journal reviews that I've kept in my files. The following is taken from an article entitled "In the World of Human Thought." The original Russian source of the review and its writer are irrelevant:

> A blindfolded man leans over a chessboard with intense concentration. He confidently picks up a figure and places it on the appropriate square. With another move he checkmates his imaginary opponent. It should be added that the victor has never played chess before, which is the whole point of the demonstration.
>
> But don't rush, dear reader, to reach a hasty conclusion. Only after becoming acquainted with the psychological experiments of Wolf Messing — a man with highly trained senses — can you see how it's done.
>
> Without outside help, Wolf Messing would never have been able to checkmate his imaginary opponent. He needs an inductor — that is, a person capable of giving him mental commands and with whom he is in immediate contact. This person holds Messing's wrist firmly in his own hand and it is he who must play chess. During the session he remains silent as a clam and can even turn his back on the psychologist after examining the board. But he must mentally suggest to Messing what his next move should be.
>
> How does Messing guess the thought of his sender? How does the physical contact between them transform the sender's nonmaterial thoughts?

I. M. Sechenov and Ivan Petrovich Pavlov have established that certain reflexes lay at the base of the brain's activity. These reflexes continually "interact" with the external environment.

For example, say you are thinking about a foot race that is due to begin in a minute. Your heart will already begin pounding faster, thereby pumping extra blood into your legs. Or say you are maneuvering on a gymnast's horizontal bar and focusing on your equilibrium. If you begin to sway and fall, your brain will correct your balance.

These scarcely perceptible motions, produced by the power of thought, represent what is termed "ideomotor" activity. These same barely perceptible motions are invariably produced by the sender or inductor, and they serve as the primary source of Messing's information.

Some people who have witnessed Messing's psychological experiments believe that he can actually receive the sender's mental commands even from a distance, but this isn't true. If Messing does seem to be able to guess the commands of his sender from a distance, it is only because he possesses a unique ability to transport the state of another person onto himself.

Now, how that differs from telepathy is a mystery to me! Messing's performances included some effects not easily explained by the "sensory cuing" theory, since they focused on the transmission of generally abstract thoughts. In order to illustrate this point, I would next like to cite an excerpt from an article that appeared in the Russian magazine *Health* in 1963. The reporter is Professor G. I. Kositsky.

Many years ago I attended one of Wolf Messing's performances. The master-of-ceremonies announced that Messing would carry out any task suggested by the audience. They were to be written out and passed up to the stage and to the panel, which had been randomly selected from those attending the performance. The jury was there to ensure the secrecy of what was written and to see that the tasks were correctly carried out. Messing didn't need to see the notes, for he could grasp their contents mentally.

Silence, which accompanies any mysterious act, settled in the auditorium.

I personally sent a note to the panel with the following text: "Remove the extra chair from aisle thirteen and place it on stage. Extract two certificates from the pocket of the girl sitting in the sixteenth seat of the tenth aisle, and add the number on the first and the validation number on the second. From the other pocket, take money equal in amount to the sum figure, and place it beneath the left front leg of the chair that was carried on stage."

I was invited on stage, and Messing asked me to take him by the wrist and concentrate on the task.

The floodlights were blinding. I held his hand while he stood next to me. Suddenly he darted from the stage and into the auditorium, dragging me with him. He walked up to aisle thirteen, feverishly grabbed the chair and returned with me to the stage. The hall filled with applause.

Feeling more at case now, I decided to begin my own experiment. I realized that my hand, which had squeezed Messing's wrist, was out of my control, so I deliberately relaxed my muscles and concentrated on the task I was trying to mentally convey.

From the audience's standpoint, it must have been an amusing scene. One person stood rooted to the spot with a frozen countenance, the other trembling nervously.

Messing shook with a slight tremor, as if a nervous tick moved from one part of his body to another. Then he suddenly froze for an instant. Then again his muscles began their nervous dance. I deliberately let my hand remain lifeless.

"Don't think about yourself! Don't think about yourself!" Messing said quietly while frozen motionless.

He was wrong; I wasn't thinking of myself at all. I was concentrating so hard on my task that I had ceased to notice anything around me.

I realized then that my thoughts could not be directly conveyed to him; he picked them up only through the vibrations of my hand. He made scores of seemingly random movements in order to evaluate my reactions to them.

If he moved by chance in the proper direction, I responded in a particular way.

This phenomenon does not entail thought transmission, but a kind of guessing. Messing was interpreting the tiny movements my hand was making. l began to lightly squeeze his wrist every time he moved in the right direction.

Messing came to life, so I repeated this light squeezing each time he moved in the right direction. He found the girl in the tenth row and brought her up to the stage, even though I had not requested it. He made countless passes over her, and when his hands were near her pockets, I again squeezed his hand lightly. At that instant he took the contents out of her pockets and placed them on the table. In the twinkling of an eye he touched every object consecutively and once more my hand tightened when he got to the certificates. After a second's hesitation, the certificates were set aside.

On the basis of this performance, Kositsky concluded that Messing's powers bore no relation to anything paranormal. His article continued:

I have not witnessed the performances of other telepaths so I will not undertake to pronounce judgment on them, but, as far as Messing is concerned, I must emphasize that there is nothing mysterious and incomprehensible about his experiments. Our thought is a product of the brain and cannot exist apart from it or from nature.

I have extensively quoted Kositsky's article in order to be fair about Wolf Messing and the controversy surrounding his performances. A few years later my son told me Kositsky was the head of the physiology department of Medical Institute No. 2 in Moscow, where he was studying. Apparently, the professor never deviated from the dogma and theories of Pavlov and Sechenov.

I remember well how I first came across Kositsky's article. As a pupil of both medicine and photojournalism, I was interested in the magazine *Health* and always tried to pick up the latest edition. One morning in March, 1963, I bought a copy at the Metropol Hotel and immediately sat down in the small public garden by the Bolshoi Theater to glance through it. After running my eyes over the contents, I instantly turned to Kositsky's piece. A half-hour later, I was tearing toward Messing's apartment.

"What is this, Tanya, showing up at the crack of dawn?" Wolf grumbled when he opened the door. I could tell that he was only pretending to be annoyed. His eyes gleamed with kindness and he looked like an overgrown child. He was fresh out of his morning shower and, with a towel draped turbanlike around his head, he looked like an Indian sage. The image would have been complete were he only holding a smoking hookah, but instead, the usual detestable Kazbek cigarette drooped from his mouth.

I handed Wolf the journal open to Kositsky's article and asked him to read it immediately and tell me what he thought. Wolf was in no hurry, though, and began pouring tea made from dogrose berries. Only after we drank a second cup did he pick up the magazine.

"Well, what can I say, Tanya?" he finally said. "You know that I never try to surround my experiments with an aura of mysticism. The professor is approaching the problem from another angle. I would agree with him if he could explain just *how* he 'signaled' me to add, not subtract, or to subtract me first number from the second.

"He didn't confuse me by letting his hand go limp, but by concentrating on himself, on his own body, instead of on the task. I deliberately brought the girl on stage so that everyone could see what I was doing.

"Professor Kositsky is not the first person who's tried to throw a cog into my wheels. Sometimes these people warn me in advance of their intentions, but, in every case, the scientists I've come in contact with have tried to ignore everything that doesn't fit into their sensory cuing theory. I can assure the professor that his attempt to not prompt me did not interfere with my capabilities.

"Of course, the fact that this gentleman wasn't thinking of the task did create some interference, rather like the static used to jam a radio signal, so I changed to another wavelength. I told him to *not* think about himself, trying to return his focus to the task at hand; I had to put him in his place like a disobedient child.

"Sometimes an entirely different type of interference can hinder me during experiments. I'm not able to telepathically 'hear' everyone with the same clarity, but of course I'm not really hearing: it is more a matter of sensing another person's thoughts and desires as my own. If my sender imagines that he is overcome by thirst, for example, then I also want a drink. If he imagines himself petting a furry kitten, my palm feels a soft little bundle.

"But as I just said, I don't really 'hear' the thoughts and feelings of every sender with the same clarity. Some are loud and others are muffled, barely penetrating through to me. Remember that I don't choose my inductors during performances. The public picks them for me.

"If I get a sender with a quiet voice, so to speak, and someone nearby is concentrating on the same psychic wavelength to which I am attuned, it can interfere with my work. The second person will drown out the thoughts of the first. Whoever has seen me in such a situation will recall that I banter jokes with those unintentional senders who probably do not understand what is happening."

Wolf got up from the table and walked over to the bookcase, near the cage of his pet canary Levuska. He proceeded to take down an enormous blue folder.

"Here's an interesting article," he said as he turned to me. "It hasn't been published yet, but the author was kind enough to send me a copy in advance."

Here are some of the most impressive parts of the report, written by Vladimir Safonov:

The following events took place last autumn in Moscow at the House of Medical Workers, where Messing demonstrated his abilities to a group of workers. I accidentally wound up as a member of the panel, and this situation made it possible for me to carefully examine what was happening both on the stage and among the spectators.

Messing's next to last experiment consisted of his performing a task mentally dictated to him without contact with the sender's hand.

To tighten the conditions, Messing was removed from the hall by two members of the panel. During his absence an object was selected and hidden in the room for Messing to find upon his return. After some heated discussions, the object — a pen — was hidden behind the wall paneling.

Messing was led back on stage. The audience froze, but Messing immediately headed right toward the girl who had hidden the pen and brought her onto the stage. He looked her intently in the eyes and demanded:

"Think! Give a mental image!"

Suddenly a mischievous thought entered my mind: What if I were to try to confuse Messing? So I immediately began to suggest to him the following: "Don't listen to the girl. The pen is not where she thinks it is. It's on the top of the column to the left of the wall."

While I was concentrating I cast only a fleeting glance at Messing, who was ten feet away from me. "The pen is on top of the column," I persisted in thinking.

To tell the truth, I didn't expect what subsequently took place.

Messing cast an angry burning glance in my direction and said with irritation:

"I don't need your superfluous commands. It would be difficult to climb up there, since there's no ladder."

I, of course, became extremely embarrassed and began to mutter something to justify myself. I stopped generating false signals right away.

Messing began concentrating again, and one could sense that he was going inside himself. He stood suspended in that manner for several minutes.

When I had finished reading the copy, Messing said, "So, Taibele, I found the pen without difficulty, of course. But I've given you this to read so that you can appreciate the difficulties I have to overcome at times.

"Sometimes the public will hinder me unconsciously; their stray thoughts echo like a discordant chorus. In order to penetrate through to the thoughts of the inductor, I have to screen out this continuous hum. It is like being at a market place, where all the merchants are vying with each other by shouting out their wares. You turn your head left and right, but you can't tell where any one voice is coming from.

"The contact with the sender's hand lightens the task and

helps me distinguish the one *essential* thought I must respond to from the others. And that is all.

"But I can easily make do without such a beacon. By the way, when my eyes are bound, the task becomes easier, and I can completely switch to the inductor's vision. There is less interference when I rely on visual perceptions than mental influences. Many think I can walk easily and freely around the hall with my eyes bound because I had instantly memorized the room's configuration, but, in point of fact, a bridge comes into being between my optic nerve and that of my sender, and I can see everything that the inductor perceives."

Wolf returned the magazine to me, signifying that our discussion of Kositsky's article was finished.

"How about some more tea?" he asked. "I want to treat you to some quince jam I received the day before yesterday from some friends in Baku."

I willingly agreed to stay, because a ticklish question preoccupied me.

The quince jam from Baku was a rare delicacy. It's long been the custom in Russia to drink either vodka or tea endlessly, and jam and sweets seem to go together with conversation.

At an opportune moment I asked my mischievous question: "Tell me, Wolf, does your audience ever send you morally questionable interference? I'm thinking of immodest or even downright indecent suggestions. Some spectators come to the theater a little tipsy at times, or they might simply want to give you a task you wouldn't dare perform, only to accuse you of fakery when you refuse to perform it. Have you ever had to deal with such incidents?"

"Tanya, you are correct when you call this sort of thing interference," Wolf replied. "The panel does not accept any obscene tasks, but in the concluding part of my performance that sort of thing can and does sometimes occur. I remember one incident in particular."

One panel received the following instructions: Wolf was to approach the fifth row, ask the woman in seat number thirteen to give him a book in a blue binding, open it to page twenty-eight, read the seventh line from the bottom, and shake her hand.

"The task was not particularly complicated," Wolf continued. "It was like thousands of others I've performed. On this occasion, seat number thirteen was occupied by an extraordinarily attractive young lady wearing a colorful dress with a low neckline. Now, the joker who sent the note up to the stage had other, definitely more amorous, things in mind than what he'd written down.

"Psychoanalytic theory holds that there are no accidental slips of the pen or the tongue. It also teaches that all words have associated, as well as literal, meanings. In this respect the words *to ask* and *to open* have hidden sexual connotations. Nor were the figures written in the note randomly selected. The person I was to approach was twenty-eight years old, and the author of the note was thirty-five. This sum is easily obtained by adding twenty-eight (the page number) and seven (the number of the verse). The word *bottom* especially gives the author away.

"Not everyone is convinced by this type of psychoanalysis, and there are skeptics even among Freud's followers. I was not acquainted with the subtle nuances of Freudian theory at the time; I simply 'heard' the young man's true intentions when I carried out his task.

"Evidently, he had met this charming young lady earlier but had not won her favor and felt rejected. It's possible that he saw her shortly before the beginning of the program, or in the lobby during the intermission.

"I stepped past the floodlights and into the half-dark auditorium. Although they didn't interfere with my telepathy, I clearly perceived his frivolous desires. These desires were clearly more important to him than his stated task. His signals unmistakably said: take off her blouse ... kiss her on the lips ... put your hand on her breast ... bend down and lift up the edge of her skirt from below...

"I heard these instructions three or four times. I read the verse from the book — a small volume of Tiutchev's poems. Finally, I told the audience, 'I will not carry out the other desires of this impudent young man. This is not the place for a rendezvous, and he should express his feelings toward this lovely young woman in a suitable manner. I am offering a session of psychological experiments, not organizing a strip tease show.' The hall resounded with laughter and applause.

"In general, Tanya, it's easier for me to perform before a sympathetic audience, the same way it is for a magician, actor, or another performer. The opening of the program is always difficult for me because I have to test my mental state and try to win the audience over. I therefore begin with relatively simple tasks, and only undertake more complicated ones when I've developed the appropriate rapport with the audience."

Over the years I have saved sets of instructions sent to Messing during his performances. When I told him that I was collecting material on his life and work, Wolf graciously assembled some of the most characteristic and frequently encountered requests submitted to him. Messing himself chose the following sets of instructions for inclusion in this book:

1

1. From the right side pocket of my suit, pull out a calendar for the year 1964.

2. Open it up to the month of December.

3. Underline today's date — November 19.

4. From the left side pocket of my suit, pull out a black packet with photographs.

5. Find among the photographs a picture of a young man and woman holding a shoe brush, and another picture of a young girl in a lavender dress.

6. Put the rest of the photographs back in the left side pocket of my suit.

7. Find the young man and woman in the fifth row, and bring them on stage.

8. From my left pant's pocket, pull out a packet of playing cards and spread them out in the following manner:

a. all the aces in one pile face side down.

b. in the upper row, the queen of diamonds, queen of hearts, leave a space for the queen of spades, and then the queen of clubs.

c. in the lower row, the kings: the king of diamonds, king of hearts, leave a space for the king of spades, and then the king of clubs.

9. From the left side suit pocket of the young man on stage, pull out the king of spades, and from underneath the young woman's right sleeve, the queen of spades.

10. Place the king of spades in the empty space in the row of queens.

11. Place the queen of spades in the empty space in the row of kings.

12. Take the young man by the hand and carry out his mental command as follows:

a. From the right inside breast pocket of my suit, pull out an envelope and hand it to the panel.

b. Let W. Messing ask the panel members to unseal the envelope and, in conclusion, read all the points of the above indicated tasks.

2

I like birds. Right now I have a cage of doves. I would like Messing to approach me in the auditorium, take the key to the cage from my right suit pocket, open it, pull out a white dove and carry it onto the stage.

3

I ask you to find out the name of the girl I love and give her a greeting card. Do this in the following way:

1. There is a girl sitting in the sixth seat of aisle twenty-two. Take her purse, open it, and among several books find a world atlas.

2. From the same purse, take out a red-blue pencil, sharpened on both ends, and mark the following Russian cities on page four in blue:

a. Novosibirsk

b. Irkutsk

c. Nikolaev

d. Alma-Ata

The first letters of these towns will compose the girl's name.

3. Between the last page and back cover of the atlas are New Year's greeting cards.

4. From among the cards, select the one with the green background, and write the girl's name on the side upon which the text is written.

5. Hand this card to the girl and wish her a happy New Year from me.

4

I ask that Messing carry out the following instructions while his eyes are bound. On the fire hydrant to the left of the stage is a military cap; inside is a wristwatch. Hand the cap to my friend, who is standing beside the third window to the left. Take the watch with you and hand it to the soldier sitting in the ninth row, seat 114. Take the keys from the right pocket of his shirt, and hand them to the girl who is sitting next to the sergeant on the panel. Ask her to stand up.

5

1. Bring onto the stage the following members of the audience:

a. row fourteen, seat sixteen;

b. row fifteen, seat two.

2. From the right outside pocket of the first person, extract a newspaper, and from his right inside pocket, a pair of scissors.

3. Fold the newspaper into quarters, then cut it into eight pieces.

4. Take a chair from the panel's table, and place it at the edge of the stage with its back to the audience.

5. Put a piece of the cut-up newspaper on the seat of the chair.

6. Take the briefcase from the second person and open the zipper fastener. Take a radio out of the case and place it on the panel's table.

7. Pull out the antenna and set the volume at maximum. Turn the knob to the right and wait for the music to come on.

At the sessions I attended, Wolf carried out tasks even more complicated.

I have thoroughly examined the scientific literature, pro and con, on the existence of telepathy. While I delved into this literature, it occurred to me that nature has often revealed her secrets to us through animals, and that examining the world of animal ESP could possibly throw light on the nature of Messing's great gift.

Animals seem capable of communicating with one another in many inexplicable ways. A certain connectedness characterizes the animal kingdom. It seems to me that this form of communication might be the result of telepathic interactions. Some scientists and parapsychologists point out that the more primitive a biological organism, the more it relies on intuitive faculties and other subtle forms of communication. For example, some have found that certain types of butterflies recognize and locate each other up to a mile apart. Telepathy has been proposed to explain this phenomenon, though the real explanation lies in the butterfly's keen sense of smell, which picks up chemical signals (pheromones) released by other butterflies.

Harder to explain, however, is the way two butterflies can fly in perfect synchronization.

The harmonious flight of a flock of swans, the silent movement of a school of fish, and the simultaneous drop to earth of a swarm of locusts — telepathy might explain these and many other phenomena of the animal kingdom.

Likewise, more highly evolved animals depend less on nonsensory communication. For example, the lion communicates by its roar, the wolf by scent. The tigress alerts her cubs to her approach with a soft purring. Monkeys have developed a complex system of auditory signals that can convey a range of messages from emotions to warnings. Many other mammals and birds communicate by sound, and humans, who have developed a complicated arsenal of communication devices, have even less need to rely on telepathy. Perhaps we gradually lost the telepathy once at our command from lack of use, and what remains with us today is only a rudimentary power.

If this line of speculation is correct, we still have to wonder *why* it wasn't needed. For if humankind once possessed a genuine psychic sense, didn't such power help us survive in the world? Or was it too much for us to handle?

This issue represents an important problem for science. Not every person would be capable, for example, of enduring the mental torments of clairvoyance. Suppose someone were able to foresee the death of a friend or some other catastrophe. He might even be aware of his own time of death. How would that person deal with such information? The psyche refuses to acknowledge our inherent mortality. Although everyone realizes that we can only live a limited period of time, the uncertainties surrounding the limits of this time create the illusion of physical immortality. Otherwise, our earthly existence would be torture, turning us into condemned prisoners waiting for execution.

Some people *can*, however, see into the future with the sixth sense. Other individuals can pick up simple telepathic impressions. Haven't you ever suddenly turned around on the street or an escalator, feeling that someone was staring at you? And someone really was?

Clearly, nature has judiciously distributed this powerful gift to only a small number of people, to keep order in the world. It is no secret that man, the often thorny crown of nature's efforts, can use his mysterious powers for evil as well as good. Fortunately, nature grants her gifts to such people as Wolf Messing, who only uses them to help his fellow man.

I remember a certain evening in Wolf's cozy little apartment on Novopeschanaya Street. He was in a particularly good mood, and, when I asked the reason, he related the following story. He had received a call from the manager of Mostorg, one of Moscow's largest department stores. Wolf had never met him, but the manager introduced himself as an ardent admirer who tried never to miss any of Wolf's performances in the city, and thanked him effusively for his help in preventing a major theft in his store. The manager wanted him to come to the store for a reward. With characteristic humor, Messing responded that April Fools' Day was still far off, and that he had done nothing to warrant the man's appreciation. The manager proceeded to give Wolf a thorough account of the "role" he had played in the escapade.

A few minutes before collecting the day's receipts, each department turned over its cash to the head bookkeeper, whose office was located beside the employees' entrance. Having filled several sacks with money, the bookkeeper turned aside for a moment to turn off a boiling teapot. In the twinkling of an eye, someone stole a sack. Clearly, the thief was an employee, since only staff used that particular passageway. But the enormous four-story store employed several hundred workers, and scores of them scurried along the service corridor at preclosing time. Suspicion could fall upon anyone — from the janitors to the forty department heads.

The petrified bookkeeper informed the manager of the theft. With the instincts of a Sherlock Holmes, he immediately sized up the situation. Only a few minutes had passed since the theft, and the bookkeeper's office was on the fourth floor. In such a short span of time, there was no way the money could have been carried outside the building. The thief could not have escaped by the stairs or by the escalator, which was jammed with customers. This meant that either the thief still had the money on his person, or that it was concealed somewhere amidst the store's merchandise.

At that moment, the loudspeaker rang out. "Citizens!" the manager said. "The bold theft of a sack of money has just taken place in our store. By fortunate coincidence, *Wolf Messing* — of whom you all know — happens to be present among our customers. I have ordered that all exits be shut off, including the employees' exits. We have no right to search a thousand people when only one person is guilty, but on your way out Wolf Messing will take your hands, one by one, and bid you goodbye. I don't think that there is any need to clarify what will happen to the thief. Therefore, I suggest that the person who, perhaps inadvertently, took the money surrender it without delay."

Within five minutes the bag was found, its contents intact, in a third-floor storeroom.

"Do you know what I just thought, Tanya," Wolf said as he finished the story, "maybe I should offer this store manager the role of master-of-ceremonies at my performances. What do you think? Even the All-Russian Theater Society doesn't provide me with such publicity." He laughed childishly.

"What about the reward?" I asked. "Are you going to accept it?"

"You and I will go together, Tanya," he responded. "But not for the gift. I'm curious to meet this quick-witted person, and we'll buy something unusual for you. He won't deny us anything! I know these merchants; they always have some hard-to-find items hidden under the counter."

"Is this the first time you have worked at such a distance, or has justice been served like this before?" I asked, keeping up the conversation, although I'll admit that, in my feminine weakness, I was already mentally preparing for a shopping spree.

"Well, I don't know of any cases," Wolf replied, "which is why I was so startled. But possibly somewhere, someone has used a similar trick."

I suddenly remembered an incident in which Wolf Grigoryevich helped to soothe some people while remaining off-stage.

In the spring of 1964, we flew together to Alma-Ata. Messing was touring through Kazakhstan, and I had a reporting assignment to finish. Approximately four months before, a crash involving the same flight killed 107 people. When this sort of thing happens, the number of passengers on subsequent flights of the same route abruptly diminishes. This is especially true, considering the human penchant for superstition, if the flights retain the same number. But people have to take the "unlucky" flights to meet their schedules, and some are nervous and fidgety, creating an unpleasant atmosphere for the other passengers.

Such was the situation on our flight. After passing candies to everyone, the stewardess disappeared behind the door of the pilot's cabin and announced over the intercom: "Attention passengers! I ask all of you to be absolutely calm. I am sure that our flight will be without incident. The famous Wolf Messing is a passenger today. He would never have come aboard an ill-fated airplane, because he can not only foresee complications down on the ground, but up in the clouds as well! The crew wishes you a happy flight and a comfortable landing."

Messing was terribly flattered by the stewardess's good-natured speech. Screwing up his eyes, he sprawled in his seat and purred cheerfully.

The passengers livened up. All started talking at once, joking about the speech and obviously relieved!

11

In the Arms of Morpheus

When plunged into an artificially induced sleep, a person becomes a toy in the hands of a hypnotist. He can be forced to recall events of years ago, forgotten either on purpose or by lapse of memory. The hypnotist can force his subject to recoil from alcohol or tobacco. Incredible things happen when a person enters a hypnotic state. Despite the power of suggestion, however, most people can be placed in this state only with their implicit permission, and when they are genuinely interested in the outcome of the session.

Luckily, most gifted hypnotists use their gift to help those in distress, not to control people for their own needs.

In 1841, the British surgeon James Braid undertook a scientific study of hypnosis, which he thought was a special form of normal sleep. He initially called it artificial sleep, but later introduced the present term, hypnosis, based on the Greek word for sleep. Modern-day physicians and law enforcement agencies frequently rely on hypnosis. The power of suggestion can help cure the ill or restore the memory of witnesses in shock.

Since many individuals are born hypnotists or learn the ability, it's not surprising that Wolf Messing practiced it also. We talked about hypnosis.

"Until now I have spoken to you about pure telepathy,"

Messing said. "Now I want to talk about another of my talents, connected with hypnosis.

"My skill in hypnotism somewhat exceeds the boundaries of its known laws, and I can't help but share some of my secrets. While telepathy is still shrouded in mystery, hypnosis, although not yet completely understood, is a power potentially available to everyone. Its mechanisms have been examined in great depth.

"I won't go into detail about the history of the subject, or how it gradually won scientific acceptance; suffice it to say that its roots are in the beginnings of human civilization.

"The priests of ancient Egypt and Greece relied on hypnotism, and in those distant times, it could not help but inspire mystical fear in the people. The dances of Eskimo shamans represent a peculiar form of hypnosis; they heal ailments in their tribes by using all kinds of spells implemented by hypnotic suggestion.

"The famous healing sessions of Franz Anton Mesmer, who worked miraculous cures in the latter eighteenth century, used nothing more than hypnosis.[*] His hypnotic power was so great that some people thought they could be totally healed just by holding an object touched by him.

"By the way, Leonid Vasiliev conducted several experiments with three women hypnotized at a distance. They never saw or heard the hypnotist, who remained in another room. They fell asleep and awoke by his silent commands; special instruments[**] confirmed this.

"Some experts distinguish three stages of the hypnotic trance. The first is drowsiness. A person in this stage of hypnosis experiences general limpness, an unusual heaviness in the body, and his eyes begin to close involuntarily. The second stage constitutes the first true level of hypnosis proper, hypotaxia, in

---

[*] Franz Anton Mesmer (1733–1815) was a Swiss physician who, in the 1770s, "discovered" a form of healing related to hypnosis based on making "magnetic" passes over patients' bodies. — editor's note.

[**] For more information, see Leonid Vasiliev's *Experiments in Distant Influence.* First published in 1962. New York: Dutton, 1976.

which the body becomes waxen and flexible. The body can be placed in any configuration, which is no problem for a person in this state, but otherwise extremely difficult to maintain.

"While hypotaxia in general is considered the second level of hypnosis, I personally consider it part of the first level only, easily achieved by people readily hypnotized.

"The third stage of hypnosis is somnambulism, in which the hypnotized subject becomes totally cut off from the external world. His only link is his subordination to the commands of the hypnotist.

"During hypnosis, the word of the hypnotist wields enormous power over the subject's mind and body. This power of suggestion completely overtakes the subject's will.

"Force yourself, for example, *not* to feel the burn caused by the tip of a lighted cigarette when it is placed against your arm! I witnessed this cruel demonstration more than once in Poland. Or, to the contrary, an ordinary pencil can be made to feel like a burning hot steel rod when placed in contact with your skin. And the marks of a real burn will remain afterward!

"You can tell a subject to put his hand on a pitcher of water and feel the cold. Even if the water is well above freezing, say, one hundred degrees Fahrenheit, the subject's hand will become covered with goose bumps as the blood vessels constrict. This is not only apparent to the eye, but can be registered by scientific instruments.

"As I have said, the underlying mechanisms of hypnosis have been sufficiently studied by science. The hypnotic state is induced by a blocking in the cortex of the cerebral hemispheres. Let's say that a person loses the power of speech through a powerful fright or some nervous shock, and his tongue and larynx are no longer under his conscious control. An instantaneous dysfunction has occurred in that portion of the cerebral cortex controlling speech. But under the influence of a new and more powerful stimulus, this portion of the brain can be unlocked.

"Recently, the world press circulated a sensational story of a deaf and mute man who regained his ability to speak and hear after being struck by lightning. Another recorded case tells of a blind man who regained his sight after a stroke.

Sometimes a talented hypnotist can artificially produce similar curative shocks through suggestion.

"How do I employ hypnosis, and what forms of suggestion do I master? I will share a professional secret with you. That incident on the train, when the conductor mistook a scrap of paper for a ticket, was a form of telepathic hypnotic suggestion.

"Let me cite a case from a later period in my career. Once I was summoned to the Kremlin by Stalin, who had heard of my escapades and was particularly interested in how I succeeded in subduing those Gestapo guards. Stalin had such a high opinion of himself, he could not believe anyone could make a fool of him.

"'You, Comrade Messing, will not be able to leave this building without this pass, signed by my secretary!' he told me. His bold assertion awoke my spirit of mischief.

"'Without this paper?' I replied defiantly. 'Keep it for yourself, Comrade Stalin, and threaten them with the severest punishment if they dare to miss me.'

"I finally managed to pique Stalin's curiosity. He dialed the number of the guard commander and ordered him not to let me through without an exit pass, which had to be marked with the exact hour and minute and personally signed by him. Next he instructed his secretary to follow ten paces behind me, but without giving any indication that he was deliberately following me. I prepared myself to enter my deepest state of trance.

"Several minutes later, I walked right out onto the street past the guards, who remained standing at attention and looking up at the window of Stalin's study. 'Maybe I should blow him a kiss,' I thought mockingly, when I glimpsed his figure by the window.

"The boundary between what is and is not morally acceptable complicates experiments such as this one, however. Each person possesses his own moral code, which serves as his finest spiritual resource. It is a code that should never be breached, even under hypnosis, or else the subject will be traumatized.

"Some experts believe that, while hypnotized, a highly moral individual will not carry out any act contradicting his beliefs. I don't know. Perhaps this power to resist hypnotic suggestion exists in some rare people, but they are probably the exceptions to the rule. "I once read of a case in which a pistol, loaded with blanks, was placed in the hands of a hypnotized subject, who was ordered to shoot at a live target. The subject did not obey. But the hypnotist could have circumvented the problem by suggesting to the subject that he was really only shooting at a target in a firing range. This is the danger of hypnosis used by psychopaths or criminals.

"Let's look back to the episode of my first telepathic suggestion to the conductor. It dulled his reasoning ability and actually induced him to transgress the rules. Hypnosis also played an important role in a bank robbery in a certain Western country. The crime was the work of a truly demonic character.

"The bank's money and valuables were stored in an underground vault, and access to it was past a check point guarded around the clock. The off-duty guards relaxed in a tiny room nearby drinking coffee, playing cards, bragging and gossiping.

"One evening after the bank closed, the safes were sealed as usual, and the cashiers departed for home. The only person left with access to the depository at that hour was the elderly floor polisher. After completing his work in the guard room, he descended to the bank's underground steel safes. Completing his work there he returned to the passageway, exchanged a few words with the guards, finished his cigarette, and left.

"The next morning found one of the safes cleaned out. The elderly janitor, a worker of many years standing who seemed honest, had been involved in another questionable incident and so suspicion fell on him.

"Two days before the robbery, the elderly man evaded customs laws and left the country for a short time with a bribe from the real thief, who asked him to be absent from work for a few days. The janitor received only a small salary, and the bribe was tempting. He of course knew that his benefactor's motives were far from pure, but he did not feel that he was doing anything illegal. During the janitor's two-day absence, the real thief substituted for him, hypnotically suggesting to the guards that he was the bank's permanent employee. Naturally, he didn't clean up the floors, but he did clean out the safe."

Everyone has heard the expression "don't sweet talk me." The Russian equivalent is "don't put a spell on my teeth." This expression comes from the countryside where, in the old days, there were no dentists. People with toothaches were healed by special spells. Local folk healers visited their patients, mumbled some words over them, and their teeth stopped aching. Rather, the person would stop feeling the pain.

Everyone has read or heard stories about folk healers who can stop blood from flowing, or who have helped individuals miraculously recover from all sorts of serious illnesses. Now, I am perfectly well aware that the power of folk medicine has an earthy origin in the power of suggestion. I was always interested in how Wolf appraised these healers. During one of our subsequent conversations, Wolf compared their feats to hypnosis.

"These spells, undoubtedly based on a form of hypnosis, take only a few seconds to utter. I know this firsthand, because I can 'sweet talk' headaches away with the touch of my hand. I've done it thousands of times, but I don't use incantations.

"My folk healing abilities are not pure panaceas, however. Folk healers take away toothaches, but our skills won't eradicate the primary cause of the pain. After we do our work the patient should seek medical treatment. Still, I feel that medical science should be more open to folk medicine and healing. Some of these practices are ancient, and ignoring them is foolish. How many secrets there are in the folk traditions of the world's cultures! Who knows, for instance, the real method by which the famous Damascus steel was prepared? These dark-patterned dagger blades gleam in their museum exhibition cases, but the secret of the steel has never been completely discovered. Also, there is an ancient column of unrusted iron in Delhi. Where can you find unalloyed nonrusting iron in the world today? We remain captivated by the eternal freshness of the wax paints used by ancient Egyptian artists, but far from everything is known about them, either. These are only a partial list of all wonders that have been irrevocably lost to us. Much superstition pervades folk medicine, but we mustn't reject it all.

"Science fiction writers have often anticipated the great scientific discoveries of the future, for example, Jules Verne's submarine 'Nautilus,' and his literary 'invention,' the hot air balloon.*

"More astounding is the wisdom of the ancients, who at times foresaw global events that took place thousands of years later.

"An Indian epic written almost two thousand years ago describes cosmic flight, telepathic communication, and mysterious sky travelers flying about in what we would today call flying saucers. There's also a three-thousand-year-old Japanese tale suggesting the theory of relativity. It tells of a young fisherman who, as a reward for saving the life of the turtle-daughter of the sea king, was allowed to spend three days in his underwater kingdom. Upon returning to the surface, the fisherman discovered that he had been away from earth, in a different dimension, for seven hundred years. I wonder if Albert Einstein ever read this tale?

"It really is true that there's nothing new under the sun! At times, we seem too willing to laugh at the revelations in common folk tales and legends."

---

* This isn't technically true, since hot air balloons date back to pre-Revolutionary France. — *editor's note.*

12

Messing Serves
as a Psychologist

On one occasion, Wolf Messing not only simply related, but slowly dictated, his reminiscences to me. I have edited them only slightly. The following recollections discuss a different side to Messing's powers: his talent in dealing with psychological emergencies.

"I can control a person's will just by looking at the back of his head, and without making visual contact with him. I recall performing in a small, cozy hall in one of the ministry residences of Moscow sometime back in the mid-1950s. My audience consisted of 250 or 300 workers from the military institution, most of whom bore insignias of ranking officers, even generals.

"Everything on stage was going according to protocol. The spectators tried conscientiously and with good humor to get to the essence of what I was projecting to them by telepathy. I was trying to avoid any occultist overtones and help them understand the experiments.

"Suddenly, at the back of the hall loomed the figure of a man, a fat, bald man with a large, protruding stomach who bore the rank of lieutenant-general. Everyone stood up and saluted him servilely. He headed for the first row and with unconcealed skepticism and iron said, in a low bass voice, 'All right, let's see your tricks.'

"I grew angry at this arrogant bureaucrat with his preconceived contempt.

"'Tricks? All right then, *you'll* be my inductor!'" I said. I started giving him mental commands. I walked behind him and coerced him to act in a manner totally out of keeping with his rank. He headed toward the stage dancing on one leg — three hops forward and one back. The audience froze with shock as they observed their great commander's hysterical movements and realized that I, Wolf Messing, was behind it all. All ended well, because the general did not know what he had been up to, and none of his subordinates ever got up the nerve to tell him.

"Was it hypnosis? Yes, without a doubt. But it was a more complex form than that which occurs with a cooperative patient in a doctor's office.

"I often used hypnosis to cure psychological disorders. A certain Polish count, who had a somewhat weak, unhealthy appearance, developed a strange paranoid delusion: he thought that pigeons were building a nest inside his head. The medical consultants didn't know how to treat this fantastic obsession. The count himself obstinately refused treatment, afraid that if he were operated on, his head would be removed along with the pigeon's nest. Having finally exhausted all possibilities, the doctors turned to me.

"I employed a completely different method of dealing with the patient. I clearly saw that it would be useless to use common sense in this case. The count's reasoning ability was severely clouded. Playing the fool, so to speak, I entered into a conspiracy with the sick man.

"For our first meeting, I brought with me a long shiny pipe on a tripod, something like a portable telescope, complete with all kinds of little screws and wheels. I placed my instrument against the count's head and painstakingly 'scrutinized' the contents of his head.

"'Yes Count,' I said, 'you are indisputably right. There is a pigeon's nest in your head, and I'm afraid that yet other families may settle in.'

"'You see!' the Count replied. 'The others doubted. Day and night I feel them flapping their wings, and now a cat has begun sneaking up on them. Then there'll really be a rumpus! My head will fly to pieces.'

"I responded confidently, 'I can drive away your uninvited residents in such a way that they'll never return to bother you.'

"The count said he would be most grateful to me. So, once more placing the 'telescope' to his head, I loudly counted his invisible feathered residents, and told him they now had a clutch of eggs. I assured him, however, that the birds would soon leave the net, since animals dislike their intimate lives open to man's scrutiny. I said they would soon fly away to find a better, more comfortable place.

"I said goodbye to the count and drove back to my hotel. Early the next morning the count sent his carriage for me.

"'Thank you, thank you greatly,' he said when he greeted me. 'The damned birds flitted away! But the new fledglings have hatched. The old ones flew away, but now there are these new ones … and the young ones make even more noise!'

"With my miraculous telescope, I once again examined the count's forehead, confirmed the presence of the young brood, and set up a final session for the next day.

"A decisive cleaning out of the count's poor head was in order. I led three assistants, equipped with live pigeons hidden in a basket, into his garden where they sat unnoticed behind the gooseberry bushes. After binding the count's eyes with a silk scarf, I led him by the hand down to the bushes.

"'This is an important moment, Count,' I said solemnly. 'Listen carefully.' I fired a pistol shot, the signal for my assistants to let the pigeons loose. At the same moment I pulled a dead pigeon out of my pocket and thrust it into the count's hands.

"'Here, Count, I managed to kill one. The others will no

longer return. Everything is over for them.' The count saw the pigeons flying away with his own eyes, and he had a dead pigeon in his hand. He immediately buried the bird in the loose earth of the flower bed.

"The count's mind remained clear for a few years, but a well-meaning acquaintance of his, wrongly assuming that the cure was permanent, revealed the essence of my trick. Upon learning the truth, the count stood for a moment in silent horror and then, with, heart-rending cry, pressed his palms to his head. The birds had returned once again.

"I doubt whether any means could cure him a second time.

"As is perfectly well known, Sigmund Freud considered dreams to be enormously significant. His main contributions to psychology included not only his successful treatment of patients, but the method and accuracy of his diagnoses. Sometimes he asked patients to relate several dreams that struck most stubbornly in their memory. By analyzing these dreams, where the subconscious manifests itself most vividly, he delved deeply into his patients' psychic lives. Dreams are like taking a trip backward in psychological time; the patient gives his own visual representation of what happened in his early life.

"I honestly admit that I know little about this still uncharted area of the human soul and never touched upon it in my experiments. I can grasp images of past or future events, however, through another psychological apparatus, and it isn't important whether you call it telepathy, or clairvoyance, or what.

"After my death, Tanya, I entrust to you the right to do with my brain whatever you see fit, and you yourself can classify my abilities!

"The following is a striking case, one I found difficult to resolve. The incident was incredible, like something out of a nightmare.

"After one of my performances in the Urals, a twenty-two-yearold man, of average build, with refined facial features, came to my hotel room. I was extremely tired after a two-hour session on stage, but I couldn't refuse to see him. Simply by looking at him I could tell that he was suffering some great misfortune. Desperation and terrible anguish were written in his eyes. I understood instantly that he had experienced some tragedy in love.

"He had been raised in an orphanage almost since infancy, and was just a young boy when officials told him his parents were 'enemies of the people.' His father was tried and shot, and all traces of his mother were lost in the camps. He did not know his real family. He enrolled in a technical school when he was sixteen and came to work as a mechanic in a factory two years later. He lived in the local hotel while waiting for an available room in the factory dormitory.

"A young woman, just passing through town, stayed at the same hotel, and they became acquainted. She was twenty years older than he was, but looked no more than seven or eight years older. She had just been released from a rehabilitation camp.*

"A passionate romance flared between them, lasting the duration of the woman's stay, then suddenly ended. She had to leave for the capital quickly in order to restore her documents and good name. He wasn't able to see her off, nor did she want him to. Feminine wisdom intervened, bringing her back to reality. She knew that nothing could come of their affair because of the great age difference. The young man said she was relieved that her train to Moscow would pass through town while he worked his evening shift. She left no forwarding address, or any other information about herself. The impressionable youth was justifiably disturbed.

"The few days they shared were filled with the intoxication of love: they spent all their free time together, and once had themselves photographed in a city park. The photograph was a bittersweet memento, the only one he had to remind him of his love.

---

* These camps were indoctrination centers set up by the state to "treat" people with "mental problems," such as harboring social or political views contrary to the government's. — *editor's note.*

"The young man reached a trembling hand into the inside pocket of his jacket and handed me a black-and-white photograph. I was stunned. I saw the face of a very beautiful young woman, surprisingly youthful for someone of thirty-eight.

"I was so shocked by the terrible discovery I had instantly made that I became frightened of my own long silence. It felt as if the young man possessed the telepathic ability to discern my discovery. I too began to tremble.

"In my hands lay evidence that the tragedy of Oedipus Rex had been re-enacted. He didn't resemble the woman in the photograph, and there was no evidence of their time relationship, but I did not for a second doubt that I held a photograph of mother and son!

"Having heard of my abilities and my much publicized predictions, he wanted to know whether I could clairvoyantly perceive her present location. More importantly, he wanted to know whether she was mother to his child.

"Nightmarish images filled my head: I saw a woman, weary with longing for a man's caress after fifteen years in prison and labor camps, comforted in the embraces of her own son. Revealing this secret would be to condemn him to a mental breakdown, and I realized I had to tell him a noble, lifesaving lie!

"Some famous lines from the poem 'The White Veil' by Shandora Petefi immediately came to mind. Taking inspiration from the poem, I decided, for the first time in my life, on a course of deception.

"In the poem a mother, on the eve of her son's execution, bids him a final farewell and promises she will attempt to persuade the despotic king to revoke the sentence. She is prepared to pay any price, including the loss of her virtue. On the fateful morning, as they lead him to the execution, he is to look to the balcony of their house, where she will be standing. If she wears a black mourning gown, then nothing has changed . 'Know that your death is inescapable,' the poem reads. But if she comes out on the balcony wearing a white veil, then the tyrant has shown mercy, commuting the sentence at the last minute.

"The next morning he is led to his execution. A crowd fervently greets the martyr, who looks steadily toward the balcony where his mother is to appear.

"And when as the procession approaches his mother's home, he sees her; she is calm and filled with grandeur and pride, wearing a white veil. His heart rejoices, even as he is led to the scaffold. The poem then ends with these lines:

> *He smiled, even after they placed the noose around him*
> *Oh sacred lie! Full of fear*
> *That her son would falter before his execution*
> *Only a mother could have told such a lie!*

"So, summoning up my will, I tried not to give myself away as I told my visitor: 'Believe me and follow my words and advice. Your dear acquaintance married a foreigner and is now living outside of Russia. She has a child but it is not yours. Forget her. Do you have the negative of this photograph? No? That's perfect. I shall keep this if you will allow me. It will serve as a remembrance of our meeting.'

"After a long period of indecision, the young man finally agreed to give me the photo. I asked him to see me once more before my tour left town. He came about five days later looking much calmer. I was pleased to see the feverish and troubled gleam gone from his eyes.

"You know, Tanya, that I always wear my talisman, my three-carat diamond ring, but I also used to carry around an amusing little Eskimo figurine carved out of bone, given to me in Magadan during one of my trips to Siberia. I carved my initials on it with a penknife, and handed it to my guest. He thanked me warmly and left, completely, it seemed, free of his recent torment."

13

Mind Control!

Wolf benefited greatly from his trips to the East during his youth. Although Europe gave him his background in psychology, the East polished the purely practical side of his work.

During his travels through India he devoted much time to studying, becoming personally acquainted with the yogis. They inspired him to continue his experiments with the cataleptic state, which he had first discovered in his early youth. He demonstrated the power in several European capitals upon his return. Then he took a twentysix-year hiatus, not because these demonstrations were ineffective entertainment, but because they exhausted him body and soul, and because open stage demonstrations of this kind were forbidden in the Soviet Union.

In December, 1963, a select group at the Central House of Writers in Moscow invited Wolf to perform such demonstrations again. Catalepsy was of greater interest as a scientific experiment than purely as entertainment.

A little over one hundred people attended the experiment. Medical personnel, including Professor Sergeev, director of the Institute of Brain Research, were present. It was on behalf of Professor Sergeev that Messing had agreed to the demonstration. Several journalists also attended. Wolf was given the respect of a physician demonstrating an extremely complex operation for his students.

The proceedings contained an element of danger and uncertainty, so it was agreed in advance that a physician, a young psychiatrist, would attend to revive Messing if the rest faltered. After the long cessation, and at the age of sixty-four, Messing didn't completely trust his powers. Dr. Lydia Pakhomova had on hand standard medical paraphernalia — caffeine, strofantin, oxygen, and so forth. She was also capable of performing emergency heart massage.

Wolf walked out on stage, folded his hands on his chest Eastern style, and made a low bow. He announced that he couldn't guarantee success since so many years had gone by since he last entered catalepsy, and apologized in advance for any possible failure.

After standing silently for several minutes, he froze as if sunk in deep thought. He stood this way for seven to ten minutes, but his heart and life functions were operating normally. After thirty or forty more minutes, however, it became clear that Messing was in a deep trance. He seemed to become a sculptured image of himself.

The psychiatrist announced she couldn't feel his pulse. Her assistant placed two chairs on stage facing each other, and some men placed Messing's cataleptic body on top of the chairs: his heels rested on one, the back of his head rested on the other. It wasn't a pleasant sight, I'd have to say, but science, like art, requires sacrifices. The body was perfectly rigid; it could have been a wooden figure.

The heaviest man climbed on a chair and sat on Messing's stomach. Even under this pressure his body did not sag. The psychiatrist injected the muscles of Messing's neck with a large hypodermic needle filled with antiseptic solution. The subject did not react, and not a drop of blood resulted from the jab. Professor Sergeev then invited a member of the audience to come on stage and ask Messing a question.

At the time, political passions raged over a Soviet-Chinese border dispute, and someone asked Messing if tensions would escalate into a military confrontation, perhaps of a global scale. He repeated the same question several times, but Messing remained silent. Someone suggested it might be possible to receive a written answer from him if a pad was placed on his stomach and a pen in his hand. The question was asked again.

In a jerky, robotlike movement, Messing raised his hand and wrote: "There will be peace!"

With that flourish, the session ended. After a few medical ministrations, Messing returned to the real world. Clearly, the session drained him.

A few days later Wolf celebrated the New Year with our family. It was obvious how trying that evening had been for him. We never saw Messing so despondent and taciturn, especially on such an occasion.

During this period, my sons were growing up and becoming independent — a simultaneous source of joy and apprehension for me. My eldest son, Vladimir, after graduating with honors from high school, successfully completed his study of theoretical physics at Bakhu University. At the age of twenty-six, he defended his candidate's dissertation, and later, his doctoral dissertation.

By 1965 Sasha had simultaneously completed premedical school and evening college, which is roughly equivalent to a U.S. high school. Although physically quite demanding, there was a definite reason for his plan. Getting into medical school in the Soviet Union has always been difficult, but in 1965 the situation was worse than ever. Most of the applicants were born in 1947, the peak year of Russia's own postwar baby boom, and competition was keen. If Sasha failed to be accepted at the institute, he could be drafted into military service. A diploma from the premed school and a graduation certificate from the college made it possible for him to apply to both of Moscow's medical schools, the Sechenov Institute and the Pirogov Institute.

On the morning of August 8, two hours after failing his first exam in chemistry and napping on a public garden bench outside the Pirogov Institute, Sasha passed his physics exam with an excellent grade. He successfully passed the examinations in all the other subjects as well. Sasha soon entered Pirogov Medical Institute, while working part time with the ambulance service.

There was no limit to my happiness. Sasha was also happy, but one storm cloud shaded his bright horizon. A certain anatomy professor, Professor Leopold Gavrilov, came to detest Sasha for some reason Sasha was never able to find out. Gavrilov always singled him out, failed him on two small exams, and made snide, demeaning comments to him at every opportunity. Once he ran into my son while he was by himself and continued his persecution.

"Lungin, you'd be better off leaving the institute," he said. "You'll never pass my subject. That I promise you."

Sasha lost his head when he heard this. He had matriculated to his second course of study, and his final exam in anatomy, his most difficult subject, was drawing near.

It seemed to me Sasha was exaggerating his poor relations with the professor, but I told Messing about the problem and that particular incident. Wolf gave me his full attention, and then suddenly began talking on a totally unrelated topic. I knew that, if Wolf diverted from a subject, nothing could bring him back to it. It appeared he wasn't in the mood to discuss the problem; the subject was never brought up again, and I figured Wolf had forgotten it.

The day of the examination arrived, a quiet, sunny day. Sasha left in an agitated frame of mind. I busied myself around the house, and had just decided to make him something special for dinner when the telephone rang.

"Taibele! It's disgraceful, understand! I can't work like this."

It was Wolf, obviously preoccupied with something. "Sasha will call. Tell him to stop fretting; he's disturbing me. Tell him that I'm with him."

"Wolf Grigoryevich, there's no way he'll be able to call," I said in amazement. "He's at an exam."

"This isn't Wolf Grigoryevich speaking, but *Messing*! He will call!"

I knew from long experience that if he made this ritualistic statement, it was useless to argue with him. I said "All right," then hung up.

The telephone rang again almost immediately. I thought Wolf was calling back to explain something, but I was wrong. It was Sasha.

"Mama, there's no use even taking the exam," he told me. "Gavrilov just walked out and in front of everybody said, 'Don't forget, Lungin, you'll be taking your oral exam with me!' You should have seen his bloodthirsty face. I don't know what to do."

I could tell by his voice that he was headed for a breakdown. I tried to soothe him.

"Wolf just called and said to tell you not to worry," I said. "He's in mental contact with you and will support you."

Sasha sighed, grateful, of course, but he found it hard to believe Wolf could help him. He decided to take the exam anyway, however.

Upset, I quickly threw on some clothes and left for the institute. Thank God it wasn't far from home; I was there within the hour. As I climbed the main staircase I saw my Sasha coming down. His face was the color of his white lab coat. He nervously told me that he got a "B." I couldn't believe it.

Sasha, transported with delight, said, "Mama, I know what Wolf can do, but *this*!" he began. "Gavrilov stared straight at me for an hour and never saw me. It was as if I wasn't there. It's a miracle! I waited for another professor to be free, a senior lecturer at the next table, and took my exam under Gavrilov's nose. I can imagine how furious he will be. Go upstairs and wait for me, and I'll be back in a flash with some wine."

Curious, I peered into the examination room. There were scores of corpses preserved in formaldehyde, used by students taking examinations. There was also a semicircle formed by five tables with teachers sitting at them. Each student in his turn proceeded to a table, where an examiner administered the test. An energetic, red-haired man sat in the center. This was obviously Gavrilov, who exactly fit Sasha's description of him. He walked out on the landing and asked the students if everyone completed the examination. A chorus of young voices answered "yes."

"Not everyone has," the scientist growled sullenly. "Lungin hasn't taken it yet."

Everyone excitedly affirmed that he did indeed complete it, and that they had seen his grade of "B." The professor raised his fiery brows in astonishment.

"How did he pass?" he demanded. "It can't be. Who gave him the exam?" The students gave him the other lecturer's name, and Gavrilov hurried into the lab to check. He returned snarling.

I realized Sasha had not exaggerated this professor's ire, and that this could have been his last examination in medicine. I also saw Wolf's psychic "hand" in this incident, and was thrilled. My son soon returned victorious, carrying two bottles of red wine. He introduced me to his classmates, and passed the wine around amid cheerful congratulations and joking. My son and I went home that day filled with happiness.

Nineteen sixty-five was a memorable year not only because of my son's success at the institute, but also because of several personal misfortunes. The major problem was my illness from radiation exposure. My condition grew sharply worse, and I was now facing hospitalization.

The experts agreed that my best chance for recovery was at a clinic for railroad workers in Moscow, where the department of hematology was headed by Josef Kassirsky, the most experienced and talented specialist in blood diseases. Being treated by Kassirsky wasn't a matter of prestige, a useless commodity in illness. Kassirsky was a truly gifted doctor, and becoming his patient was to me a matter of necessity, not honor. Unfortunately, only professional railroad workers and Communist party officials had access to the clinic. I couldn't bring myself to use my acquaintanceships with Wolf Messing or with Kassirsky himself to pull the necessary strings.

My elder son took matters into his own hands. He called the clinic, passing himself off as some magnate from the Ministry of Communications! I was accepted without delay even though the wards were crammed with patients.

Dr. Kassirsky told me firmly, a few days after the necessary tests, that surgery on my spleen was unavoidable. I could do little but agree submissively to his plans. Secretly, though, I shook with fear. I knew that the removal of a spleen was not a safe operation.

A constant reminder to us weak adults, shaking and worrying over real and imagined illnesses, was a nine-year-old child suffering from an incurable condition. The doctors said her death was inevitable, yet she steadfastly endured her sufferings. The night before my operation we sat and talked, and I forgot my apprehensions. We discussed my travels throughout the country, and I was just describing the beauty of the tundra and the Northern Lights when a nurse walked into the ward. She was very tall and masculine-looking. Many men would have envied her physique!

"Lungin, you have a call," she barked in a voice filled with irritation. "But let this be the last time. Telephone calls distract the personnel from their work. And they're always over trifles."

I answered timidly that I hadn't given the clinic's number to anyone; I didn't know it myself. I went down the hall to the telephone.

"Taibele?" the voice on the line asked. Only Wolf called me by that name.

"You have an operation scheduled for tomorrow?"

"Yes."

"Don't worry, there won't be any operation. Good night." Without further explanation, Wolf hung up. I was overjoyed, but then I remembered that Wolf hadn't said those magic words, "This isn't Wolf Grigoryevich speaking; this is *Messing*!"

The best thing for me to do, I thought, is forget everything and go to sleep. Early the next morning the same stern nurse walked into the ward and told me not to eat anything before the operation. How could this be, I thought? What of Wolf's prediction?

The whole ward grew silent in sympathy. The women looked at me dolefully as I said goodbye and followed the nurse down the corridor, past the operating room, and down to the first floor. Behind doors inscribed with the words "conference hall," Professor Michael Abramov of the hospital staff waited for us.

With an overwhelming feeling of apprehension I walked in. Inside were about two hundred doctors and students, all dressed in white. As I walked to the front I sensed their eyes following me, and felt like I was on display. Dr. Kassirsky was there, too, dressed neatly in a black suit. He took my hands and said that, on the basis of a bone marrow analysis, my operation had been postponed. He explained to the students that if the present course of treatment didn't improve my condition, the operation would be performed without delay.

Freeing myself from the physician's friendly embrace, I looked at him and asked, "Did you make the decision because of something Messing said?"

He was surprised. "Messing? What does he have to do with this?" Then he smiled and said, "No, my dear, my friends don't interfere in the affairs of my patients. Even Wolf Grigoryevich. And besides, I haven't seen him for quite a while."

I returned to the ward elated. Even though I feared the nurse's routine reprimand, I waited impatiently to hear from Messing. He and Iraida visited the next day with a big box of chocolates and some bananas.

Wolf Grigoryevich diplomatically evaded all my inquiries as to whether his psychic intercession forestalled my operation. Did he telepathically suggest to Kassirsky that it was unnecessary? Did he treat me himself? But Wolf turned the conversation away from medical topics, acting as if we were in a convalescent home rather than a clinic. I was discharged from the hospital three days later with orders to get a lot of bed rest.

This incident illustrates aspects of Moscow life that must seem odd and even contradictory to some Western readers. Particularly now, as the Russian words "glasnost" and "perestroika" become part of an international vocabulary, our existence during the Stalin and post-Stalin years appear more and more like a nightmare.

The privileges Wolf Messing enjoyed as part of a Soviet elite of performing artists, are privileges most are born into. The pattern of privileges, exchange of favors, routine deprivations, and bureaucratic neglect were simply part of our everyday reality. Books have been written about the social hierarchy that makes up Soviet society. Mikhail Gorbachev's tolerance of a degree of public criticism regarding high-level privileges has allowed the realities of our "classless society" to become more widely known.

Since Stalin's day, the highest level of Soviet society has included only Communist party leaders: the Politburo, the party's Central Committee, and various parallel governmental agencies. While dissident artists and writers were ostracized, sent to labor camps, exiled, and even executed, others were heaped with honors in the forms of privileges and decorations such as the Order of Lenin.

In terms of income, living accommodations, and travel privileges, Wolf Messing fit what might roughly be called the third or fourth level of social prominence. Prominent performers are essential to Soviet society because their skills divert audiences from the hardships of daily life or, indeed, from such horrors as Stalin's purges and the devastating war years.

We were fish, swimming in the sea into which we were born, often quite unaware of the meaning of the daily compromises, polite silences, and diplomatic phrases we uttered automatically. I was too young in the 1930s to be truly aware of the purges. Today, such pioneers of the Bolshevik Revolution as Nikolai Bukharin are finally being vindicated. It is difficult to remember, and certainly very difficult to convey to a non-Soviet audience, the almost automatic self-censorship we all imposed on ourselves. That Messing was allowed to speak to Stalin with his usual candor must have been due to the dictator's own multifaceted personality. Stalin could project uncomplicated, peasantlike simplicity, or benign "father of the country" qualities. These were the characteristics he seems to have displayed with Messing.

Messing managed to survive the many changes in Soviet society, although he remained ever sensitive to the suffering all around him. His simple life and high income enabled him to help others without drawing attention to himself or to those he helped. Many things went unsaid, because there was no use in saying them.

The Soviet Jewish community was doubly conscious of the irrational period preceding Stalin's death. The world has by now forgotten that, from 1949 on, Stalin lived in his own narrow paranoid world. Always a conspirator himself, he feared just about everyone around him, including his fellow members of the Politburo. But it was his paranoid fear of physicians, leading to his notion of a Jewish "doctor's plot" against him, that sent fear through the Jewish community during the last few weeks and months of his life. His successors quickly abandoned the notion, but those frightful months were difficult to forget.

The question in all of this is: could a man like Wolf Messing have accurately read Stalin's mind? Even more intriguing: could he have, hypnotically, telepathically, changed his devastating mind-set? The answers elude us. The answers would, in fact, only raise an even more profound issue: the manipulation of human minds by governments too intrusive, too fearsome to imagine.

14

White Water
on the Volga

There was a raging sea of people at the Central House of
Medical Workers in Moscow on January 19, 1966. Police units
were reinforced to control the unruly crowd, which consisted
primarily of people unsuccessful in obtaining tickets for Wolf
Messing's anniversary performance. He had actually turned
sixty-seven, but, for some reason, the government decided that
this would be the famous telepath and clairvoyant's sixty-five-
year jubilee.

I had spent the previous evening at the Messings and knew
that Wolf wasn't feeling too well. Iraida told me he was sure
his chronic appendicitis was flaring up. He was obviously not
pleased by these anniversary celebrations, but it was impossible to
cancel them. The public's interest in this event was too great, and
scientists, journalists, and many other important admirers were
to attend. I suggested he consult Professor Victor Agranenko,
a skilled surgeon from the Institute of Hematology and Blood
Transfusion; perhaps he needed to go into the hospital. But
Wolf obstinately refused, saying he didn't have the right to let
so many people down.

The auditorium of the Central House of Medical Workers
was filled to capacity. In order to accommodate those not

fortunate enough to obtain tickets, loudspeakers were set up in the vestibule and some adjoining locations. Famous physicists, biologists, other academicians, and journalists, sat on a dais. I sat with my sons in the sixth row, nervous about the welcoming address I was to deliver.

It's not easy to speak appreciatively about a friend in his presence and beneath the gaze of so many eyes. My speech didn't turn out the way I planned; and I simply related the story of our meetings, liberally embellishing it with flattering epithets. My last words were obscured by applause, but I was dissatisfied. Embarrassed, I walked off stage and returned to my seat. Although they were more eloquent, the other speakers didn't do much better, just addressing Wolf Messing in wildly enthusiastic terms.

Wolf politely gestured for all the speakers to remain on stage, where baskets of flowers had been arranged in a semicircle by the table. The largest was an arrangement of tulips, a gift from war hero and ace pilot Valentina Grizadubova. Messing, flattered by the warm words and attention, sat at the center of the table like a child at his birthday party. He could only say, "Friends, thank you very much!"

With these few words, he began his performance — this time with a new twist.

Right at the start, a fat woman about sixty years old, wearing a dress of heavy material and a wool scarf around her shoulders, walked on stage and announced that she had been suffering from an unbearable headache for more than six months. Messing requested a glass of ordinary drinking water, which someone poured from a crystal decanter on the dais. Wolf whispered something into the woman's ear, held her by the wrist for several seconds, and ordered her to take several swallows of water. Almost immediately she joyfully announced that the pain had disappeared!

The next day the celebration continued, but in a less official setting. Messing held a sumptuous banquet at the magnificent

Red Hall in the Prague Restaurant on Arbat Street. The distinguished guests included scholars, writers, politicians, and many others; the editor-in-chief of *Science and Religion* was also present. Few of Wolf's public debates or meetings ever took place without the presence of this magazine's tiresome representatives.

They seemed to watch him to make sure nothing occultist or mystical crept into the performances.

All passed the evening in a relaxed mood, with jokes and laughter and toasts. The restaurant employees were also pleased. Although unimpressed by the foreigners and high-ranking party officials (the Prague Restaurant had long been the favorite haunt of Moscow's elite), they were, however, fascinated by Messing. People came in from a neighboring banquet hall where an important wedding was taking place. Toward the end of the evening, the bride and groom themselves came in to ask for Messing's autograph! I am sure that the newlyweds and wedding guests were convinced the union would be long and successful, but when they returned to their banquet Wolf said quietly, "They'll live together exactly five months."

Unfortunately, I can't verify this prediction; I never met the couple again. I have no doubt, however, that Wolf's prediction was fulfilled.

When somebody offers you the secret of a get rich quick scheme for two bucks, it's an obvious con. You wonder why the promoter isn't already rich himself. A psychotic psychiatrist or a physician who can't diagnose his own flu also seem absurd. But can a gifted telepath and healer find himself in a similar situation?

The day after the celebrations Iraida called to say that Wolf had just been taken by ambulance to the Botkin Clinic. He was in critical condition and scheduled for emergency surgery. My son Sasha, then a second-year student at the Medical Institute, worked with the ambulance service for the same clinic. He was waiting for me on the front steps of the main entrance when my taxi arrived. My heart froze, for Sasha was holding up his index fingers in the form of a cross, signifying to me that the situation was grave.

He explained that Messing's appendix had burst, resulting in peritonitis. It looked like death was at his door.

Moscow was then in the grip of a flu epidemic and hospital visits were forbidden to the public; but my son told Wolf of my arrival, and I was admitted at his special request. He greeted me with a weak smile. I bent over and kissed his forehead, and I realized the effort his smile must have cost him; his fever was no less than 104 degrees. He maintained his spirits and did not complain, but his breathing was heavy and labored.

Also in this ward was a young man of Herculean stature with an Ernest Hemingway-style beard, who had wound up there through some misunderstanding. Messing intercepted my glance toward the young man, beckoned me with his finger, and whispered softly in my ear.

"Taibele, these damned doctors obviously think I'm finished," he said, "but they're wrong. I feel sorry for that young fellow, though. He's in his last days, though he appears to be in fine shape."

During my second visit, Wolf asked for some black caviar. He lost his appetite for everything else. After traveling all over Moscow, I managed to obtain about one and a half ounces of it at a small out-of-the-way restaurant, and immediately hurried to the clinic with the precious gift. Wolf was overjoyed to see both me *and* the caviar. Now he was smiling effortlessly, and I could see that things had taken a turn for the better. But the brawny young man was no longer in the ward; he died, just as my friend had foretold.

Messing also received regular visits from his stage assistant, Valentina Ivanovskaya. She was patient not only with Wolf, but also with Iraida, whose disposition and caprices often made life difficult. Surrounded with continuous care and attention, Messing quickly recovered and was released from the clinic within a few weeks with orders to remain in bed at home for awhile. The threat passed, and Messing celebrated his birthday in full health.

Since the jubilee, all arrangements for future celebrations were entrusted to me, and I was pleased to assume the responsibilities. On one occasion three years later, we held his birthday celebration in the restaurant of the Sovetskaya Hotel. Wolf Grigoryevich always loved to perform in that hotel's auditorium. Once again, many local luminaries attended. Messing was loved by everyone.

The occasion was a great one: Messing's seventieth birthday. I had secretly ordered an enormous birthday cake and barely managed to fit seventy candles on it. The guests sat down solemnly at their tables, the champagne was uncorked, and the lights suddenly went out. Wolf barely had time to grumble his predictable modest words of appreciation when I floated out of the darkness with the cake and placed it before him. The twinkling candles illuminated the room.

Messing broke into a broad smile. I could tell he was touched when he kissed me. He was strong in spirit; unfortunately, it was trapped in a rapidly weakening body.

Pandemonium broke out in Moscow during the summer of 1967. The Soviet government celebrated its fiftieth anniversary. The flood of propaganda accompanying the preparations often irritated Wolf; all theatrical and stage performances had to conform to revolutionary or patriotic themes. Since Wolf's psychological experiments didn't fit in, he took advantage of the decreased demand for his performances to relax away from the city. Some medical researchers invited Messing to the Upper Volga. Wolf had given many performances in that district, and had even given consultations to the local psychiatrists. This trip, however, was planned as a vacation.

Wolf, in turn, invited me and my sons to join him on the trip, and we accepted without a moment's delay. My elder son, involved in the unpleasantries of a divorce proceeding, was to join us later.

Messing learned of my son's marriage only after it had taken place. Vladimir dated his bride-to-be while Wolf was in the Far East. He reproached me at the reception for not consulting with him. As a friend of the family, he told me the marriage was doomed. "Exactly half a year-remember this, Taibele," he said, "it will only last half a year!" The prediction came true and we suffered the consequences.

From that time forward, Vladimir took a strong interest in his brother Sasha's affairs of the heart. He evidently feared Sasha would make the same mistake he did, and tried to gently influence his brother. Sasha developed a passion for one particular young lady, and Wolf suspected future unpleasantness. I think that's why he invited us to join him on his trip.

Messing showed up at the Kazan railroad station with someone I didn't recognize, probably a local bureaucrat secretly helping him. The next day, upon our journey's end, Messing's old friends greeted us noisily at the platform. They drove us to a boarding house in an old, beat up truck. The house was situated picturesquely on a steep bank of the Volga River, and a silvery stream made two half circles around the estate before flowing into the great Volga just three hundred feet away. The river accented the freshly hewn, yellow wooden planks of cozy Finnish cottages that gleamed in the twilight, and in the moon's radiance.

Wolf brought along his lap dogs, Pushinka and Mashenka. Released from the cramped and stuffy life of the city, the dogs raced madly around the estate from early morning until late at night. In the first minutes of our arrival, we felt how much our city lives deprived us of contact with nature.

Most of the plentiful autumn mushrooms had still not broken through the ground, but each morning, accompanied by Mashenka and Pushinka, we went to the nearby pine forests to pick those few that could be found.

Three small neglected villages, visible from the Volga's shore, formed a striking architectural ensemble with their ancient

Russian Orthodox churches. Sadly, they languished in a state of disrepair due to age and human indifference. Their injuries, however, were merely physical; they still radiated their original spiritual grandeur. They came to life in the hours before sunset, when the sun's crimson rays illuminated the remains of their gold-covered cupolas. Wolf admired the mournful but majestic sight for hours upon end.

We took our meals in a romantic setting. We descended to the shore along wooden planks outfitted with a handrail, and, in a quiet backwater, we dined on an old steamship transformed into a restaurant. It rocked lightly on its moorings, and we heard the hoarse cry of seagulls as they flew over the water's smooth surface. The tables were set with charming ceramic bowls filled with roast meat and mugs filled with an old Russian drink made from honey. The cutlery was all made of wood, and the spoons, plates, and bread dishes were decorated by Khokhloma artisans.

The restaurant workers immediately recognized Wolf Messing, and we took full advantage of them at times. We asked them to prepare the mushrooms we gathered, sometimes in a sour cream sauce, sometimes pickled. Sasha, an ardent fisherman, rarely participated in our mushroom-gathering expeditions, preferring to sit for hours at the river fishing for white-sided bream or, if he was lucky, the famous Volga sterlet. Sometimes he brought back a good halfbucket of booty; Wolf was even more excited than Sasha over his catches, and headed straight for the kitchen every time to request his favorite sturgeon soup.

During this intoxicating month of rest, Sasha grew especially close to Wolf. Wolf somehow found the right approach to closing up the tremendous age difference that separated them.

Especially enchanting were the nights we spent beside an open fire, inspiring us to tell romantic stories and fantastic tales of mystery and intrigue. Each of us would tell a story, and, when we all had our turn, we started again. I often, however, tampered with the sequence so that Wolf Grigoryevich could be story-teller most often. These campfire soirées by the Volga gave us the opportunity of hearing some stories from Wolf's fascinating life, and I would record them the following mornings. Wolf also loved sentimental stories about dogs. He exhibited a childlike purity, curiosity, and trustfulness when telling them.

The days of our vacation flew by quickly, and we began to count our remaining days with a certain sadness. But Messing was still acquiring new friends. On hot days he headed for the nearest village where, beside an abandoned mill in the leafy grove of a cemetery, a natural spring gurgled forth. He scooped up the water in his hands to quench his thirst, and he brought us back some in a plastic jug for our evening tea. He became friendly with all the local peasants during these forays, buying fresh milk from them and questioning the old folk about any once famous fortunetellers or healers from their region. Because the majority of his appearances were in cities, Messing did not get to meet peasants as much as he would have liked.

The villagers in turn grew fond of this strange lord, and several days before our departure they gave him a keepsake: a sculpture carved of wood depicting a man sitting on a barrel and drinking home brew from a large mug. The settlements surrounding Nizhny Novgorod have been famed from time immemorial for their master craftsmen. Wolf greatly valued this gift as a reminder of the wonderful days that had so healed his soul, and as the first souvenir he ever received from peasants.

We returned to Moscow feeling young and refreshed. "Who could have foretold that I would experience such bliss," Wolf said to me.

15

Witnesses Speak from America

After an excerpt from the original Russian version of this book appeared in the New York emigré newspaper *The New Russian Word*, I received calls and enthusiastic letters from many readers who considered it their duty to share their impressions of their meetings with Messing in the Soviet Union. Some told me how Messing cured them or their friends of serious ailments. Interrupting my personal story for the moment, I will relate the stories of people, currently living in the United States, who have witnessed Messing's predictions come true with astonishing accuracy.

The first was sent to me by the well-known New York journalist Mikhail Germonov:

In the beginning of 1946 in Leningrad, an announcement was made of the coming appearances of Wolf Messing with his sessions of psychological experiments. By that time, rumors of Messing's amazing telepathic abilities had even reached Leningrad. Rumors spread of how this refugee from Poland, with the aid of telepathic suggestion, had simply walked out of the cell of a Warsaw prison where he had been confined by order of Hitler's occupational forces, and of similar "miracles." At the time I was head of the theatrical section of the paper *Evening Leningrad*, and one fine day Wolf Grigoryevich Messing appeared in the editorial office accompanied by his wife and assistant, Aida Mikhailovna.

Attaching great importance to his first scheduled performance, Wolf Grigoryevich asked me to help dispel the impression that his performances were only the ordinary tricks of magicians and illusionists. He offered to give a preview before the editorial staff, right on the premises of the editorial office.

The next day after work, Wolf Messing showed up in the conference hall. We saw a man of medium height, with a shock of blue-black hair, bright, penetrating eyes, nervous, emotionally excitable.

After a short introductory address given by his wife about his telepathic abilities, Messing began a series of experiments. He located hidden objects with ease, holding his examiner by the wrist. He read the texts of notes written by employees of the newspaper. He read out loud pages from books which he had only glanced at for an instant. He instantaneously carried out an operation with large mathematical figures, solved complex problems by extracting square and cube roots from seven-figure numerals, and in addition remembered all the figures involved in the operations. In a word, everything before him had been demonstrated by the amazing Russian phenomenon *Arrgo* (L. C. Levitin) and later by his Leningrad disciple Mikhail (Hans) Kuni. Messing performed no experiments with telepathic suggestion, explaining that this was categorically forbidden by the authorities.

After the performance, while saying goodbye to me and my wife, he turned to her with the following offer: "I know what is oppressing you," he said. "You want terribly to find out the fate of a person dear to you. Come see me tomorrow morning at the Europe Hotel and I will share what I know of your doubts."

It was with some understandable agitation that my wife went that morning to see Wolf Grigoryevich. Taking her by the hand he said, "You are disturbed about the fate of your brother, who fought in the Second World War." Indeed, he *was* missing in action at the very end of the war, and none of us knew of his fate.

"Unfortunately, your brother Anatol died from an enemy bullet a few days before the end of the war." Messing even called him by his proper name.

Thus Wolf Grigoryevich definitely dispersed all our doubts about the fate of a relative, which was later documented in a communiqué we received from the municipal military registration and enlistment office. This amazing man undoubtedly had remarkable abilities.

From her home in Boston, the writer Nadeshda Filipovna Kramova told me about a more interesting meeting with Wolf Messing.

I want to tell you of several episodes that characterized his truly magical gift not only of "seeing" events occurring far away, but of foreseeing events of the future.

I met Wolf Messing during the war. Based in Perm (then called Molotov) was a group of writers evacuated from Leningrad. We lived in the only seven-story building in town, a hotel nicknamed "The Seven Story." Once while in the lobby, I saw a short man with a large head and locks of hair sticking out in all directions. Walking up beside me, he stopped, cast me a needle-sharp glance, smiled at something, and headed with quick, mincing steps toward the exit.

"Who is that?" I asked the hotel administrator.

"What, you don't know? That's Wolf Messing. He arrived yesterday," was the reply.

"Ah!" I said, ashamed to expose my ignorance. At the time the name told me nothing.

Soon, Messing held his first performance. I will not dwell on his phenomenal ability to read thoughts, or his power of suggestion. I will relate something that, for the time being, is impossible to explain.

Messing was given a rather simple task: walk up to a certain lady in the third row, take her passport from her purse, bring it on stage, and open it up. After reading the owner's name out loud, he was to return the passport. When Messing got on stage and opened the passport, a photograph fell out.

"What a handsome officer," he said with a smile. "Just a young boy."

Suddenly his face distorted, his eyes widened, and he clutched at his heart.

"Curtain! Drop the curtain!" he shouted. The hall froze.

His assistant walked out on the proscenium and announced that Messing was feeling poorly, but within about ten or fifteen minutes the session continued. The last part of the performance dragged, and Messing stopped frequently to wipe his face with a cloth. The next day we managed to find out from his assistant what had happened. Messing had "seen" the youth being killed at the very minute he was admiring the photograph.

The mother of the youth did not stay at the hotel, but we saw her every day in the cafeteria where our food ration cards were registered.

We looked with horror at her face, but it was just as calm as always; her son wrote to her often and she showed us his short, affectionate letters. In time we calmed down, figuring that Messing had made a mistake. After all, people do make mistakes.

Three weeks passed, and we forgot about this episode. But twenty-four days later, the woman did not come to the dining hall. The next day we learned that she had received a notification of her son's death, and the day and the hour of death indicated was the same day and hour Messing had "seen."

I tried never to miss any of Wolf Messing's performances. Once I lingered around after the session. The hall was already empty, and I was the last person to walk out onto the frozen street. A snow storm was raging, and nothing was visible for more than two paces in front of me. Standing indecisively at the entrance was Messing.

"Wretched weather," he grumbled in German. "Like in hell."

"Worse," I responded, "at least there it's warm."

"You speak German?" He turned and looked at me inquisitively. "That's good. You're staying at the hotel. I saw you in the lobby."

I nodded, surprised by his memory.

"Take my arm and let's go," he continued in German. "Now at least there's someone with whom I can converse in German. Russian is more difficult for me."

"But where is your assistant?" I asked.

"Sometimes she leaves after the break."

After that evening I often met him by the entrance, and together we returned to the Seven Story Hotel.

"Speak in a low voice," he warned me. "Since the war it's dangerous to speak German on the street. Once I was almost arrested as a spy." He laughed.

Those were heavy, anxious days for me. I had stopped receiving news from my husband since the siege of Leningrad. Rumors circulated that he had been killed during a bomb attack. I held out for a long time, but finally decided to turn to Messing. I didn't want to speak to him of my anxieties merely in passing, but I didn't have the courage to ask for a special audience: I knew he was forbidden to practice his skills in private. Finally, I asked his assistant to put in a word for me.

"He's agreed, as an exception," the assistant said. "Come to his room at three o'clock."

I will try to reconstruct the conversation I had with Wolf Messing word for word.

"You're here? Sit down. But keep in mind that I'm not allowed to receive visitors. Therefore, fifteen minutes and not a second more," he said.

I sat down obediently, not knowing where to begin.

"To begin," he caught my thought, "write down any number on a piece of paper." He handed me a pencil and paper. "Write. Write."

I wrote the number eighteen.

"Now fold the paper and put it inside your shoe. Like that. Give me your hand."

I obediently carried out the procedure. Within a second Wolf Messing wrote "18" on a scrap of newspaper and looked at me triumphantly. I shrugged my shoulders. It was only wasted time.

"Ha!" Messing suddenly said. "I didn't come for him to show me his tricks; it's only wasted time." He added, "Did I guess right?"

I smiled involuntarily.

"But you want to ask about the fate of your husband."

"What else do women want to know about during a war?" I thought irritatedly. "One doesn't have to be Messing to know that," I said.

"But in order to answer your question it's necessary to *be* Messing," he chimed in craftily, and then burst out laughing. He was behaving like a mischievous child, and he began to irritate me.

Suddenly his face grew serious.

"I'll tell you what," he said. "To begin with, I want to acquaint myself with your apartment — there in Leningrad." He squeezed my hand tightly by the wrist. "Walk into the entrance hall. That's it. Go slowly, to the left, the door to someone else's room, the hallway, to the right — your room, walk in. No, the piano is not by the wall next to the door, but right by the window; the glass is broken, the top is open, there's snow on the strings. Well, why did you stop? Go further. The second room is almost empty: no chairs or table either, no shelves — the books are lying in a heap on the floor in the middle of the room. Well, enough."

He dropped my hand. "And now listen carefully! Write this down!" As he spoke his face grew pale and strained. "Your husband is alive. He is ill, very ill. You will see him. He will come, he will come here — July fifth at ten in the morning. Remember: July fifth at ten o'clock!"

Messing grew silent and closed his eyes, while I sat afraid to move.

"And now go, this minute!" he said quietly. "I have a session this evening. I have to rest and here I am playing around with you!" He looked at me angrily. "I am tired. Go!" he shouted, wiping beads of sweat from his forehead .

July fifth eventually drew near. I already knew [from a relative in Leningrad] that my husband was starving, suffering critically in a hospital. There could be no question of his arrival in the Urals in the near future. But Messing's prediction never left my mind, and I and all my friends anxiously awaited this day. I even made preparations for our reunion; I acquired vodka with butter coupons, pledged part of my bread ration cards for mint candies, and traded ten feet of cotton material given to writers by the Literary Fund for potatoes and onions.

On July fifth I was alone in my room (the neighbor who had been staying with me went to another room the night before). I was afraid to go down to the dining room to eat lunch or even to go get boiling water for tea.

The hours passed: ten, eleven, twelve ... four, five, six. Every few minutes heads poked through the door. "Has he come?" people would ask.

"Not yet," I had to reply.

I sat there hungry, ill-tempered, sobbing, feeling foolish, and indignant at my gullibility.

At seven o'clock in the evening a faint knock sounded at the door. My husband stood in the doorway. On his back was a tightly-filled knapsack, and he clutched two loaves of bread to his chest.

"My God! I've been waiting for you all day!" I shouted as I ran to him.

"How did you know that I would come today?" My husband said surprised. "It happened totally unexpectedly. I had just gotten out of the hospital, and suddenly I got a call."

Tell me everything later," I responded. "I can see you're barely standing on your feet."

I took the bread from his hands and helped him take off the knapsack. If I hadn't been waiting for my husband, I wouldn't have recognized him in this old man with sparse, graying hair, sunken temples, a haggard face covered with the gray stubble. He was only forty-two years old. When we had parted not long ago, he had been handsome, elegant, and in fine physical shape. My heart sank.

"I expected you this morning," I said, "but the main thing is that you came today."

He replied, "I did arrive this morning, at ten o'clock."

"What?" I said in horror. "Where were you all day?"

"You see, at the station they handed our two loaves of bread to everyone on the train, and I stood in line for eight hours. After all, I couldn't turn down *bread.*"

"My God! I have enough bread!"

I wanted to cry but I restrained myself. Before me was a man who had lived through the siege of Leningrad, and I understood.

When I returned to my room in Leningrad, I saw the piano with the open lid by the broken window. The snow had melted and the strings were drenched with water. The floor was piled high with books in the second room. The shelves, chairs, and table were gone — the neighbors had burned them in the frozen winter in 1942. I was glad it helped them survive.

I shall pick up my story again in telling of yet another case in which Messing's predictions changed the lives of several people and helped to create a new family. My son Sasha was the key player in this little drama.

Early in 1968, Sasha became acquainted with a nice girl from Czechoslovakia whose parents were employed in the Czechoslovakian Embassy in Moscow. Soon they became very attached to one another and met practically every day. I watched with pleasure as their innocent and friendly relationship turned into love. It was frightening, however, to think seriously of the future; marrying a foreigner is extraordinarily difficult and often ends unhappily. Events in Czechoslovakia had been gathering steam, and Soviet troops had recently entered the small country. Consequently, Iva's parents — like many other Czechs — sharply changed their attitude toward everyone and everything in the Soviet Union. This was an important moment in Sasha's life, and I didn't want to see him repeat his brother's mistake. I advised him to see Messing for advice.

This was the first time we had ever directly asked Wolf for help. He invited Sasha and Iva to his home one Saturday for tea. Wolf asked them to bring a photograph of Iva's parents.

Everything worked out beautifully. Wolf was in a good mood that day and joked during the entire visit. As the couple were getting ready to leave, he told them he'd have an answer regarding their future within two days. We spent those two days in a state of unrelieved tension, fearing a negative analysis. We didn't think Sasha would have the strength to break off with Iva in such an event.

Three days later, Messing summoned Sasha to his apartment. When he returned home, he was very excited and happy and wrote down everything that Wolf Grigoryevich had said about his future with Iva.

"You must marry Iva," Wolf said. "No one will ever love you with such devotion as she will. She is a very good person. One encounters few people like her. It will be exceptionally difficult for you in the beginning. Her parents will renounce her, but within two years after the birth of your first son they will change their attitude. You will have two sons and one daughter, and you will be a very successful doctor."

Is there any need to describe Sasha's happiness?

To tell what Sasha and Iva suffered through would require a separate book. Here is what happened in brief:

Six months after this conversation, Sasha and Iva married. Their first son, Garrett, was born in December of 1969. Who knows if he would have been born were it not for that meeting with Wolf Grigoryevich? In the summer of 1971 they went to Czechoslovakia, and from that time forward their relations with Iva's parents began to improve. Their second son, Tomash, was born in 1972. In 1973 Sasha graduated from the Medical Institute.

In 1978, after we applied for exit to Israel, Iva and the children were deported as aliens to Czechoslovakia. It was only after a half year of many trials and adventures that they met again in Vienna.

After his arrival in America and three years of serious physical and material losses, Sasha finished podiatry school and, just as Wolf had predicted twenty-five years earlier, became a doctor.

No matter what trials befell my children, Messing's prediction of a successful and happy ending was always their guiding star and soothing balm.

Iva and Sasha have been living happily ever since. When

I wrote the Russian edition of this book in 1981, Sasha was thirty-four and Iva thirty-two. They had been married for twelve years and as yet had only two sons. But, sure enough, Iva and Sasha have become parents for the third time. Their daughter, born in May, 1982, thereby fulfilled Messing's prediction.

16

The Beginning of the End

The "bank robbery" in which Wolf Messing took part on Stalin's orders brings the following story to mind.

At the very beginning of the 1970s, the Soviet government began a regular public lottery called "Sportlotto." At first it was held every ten days, but later it was held daily. The first drawings, which were even shown on television, were carried out rather amateurishly with forty-nine numbered balls placed inside a drum and mixed up. A celebrated sports figure or actor would close his eyes and pull out the six winning numbers. This method naturally prompted the censure of inveterate gamblers, and even many more detached observers grumbled at the proceedings. They all suspected that the lottery was pure deception. If, several days before the drawing, the lottery commission ran every conceivable combination of numbers through a computer, they could determine in advance which would bring in the maximum winnings, and this combination would then be purportedly "drawn." Since this number would turn up only once in a million purchased tickets, there would be little risk of multiple first prizes.

There were several possible ways of fixing the results; two of them seemed rather easy. One method would be to heat the six necessary balls so that they could be easily detected by touch. Or, the balls could be chilled. The flaw, of course, is the likelihood of drawing the balls in the incorrect sequence.

The manner in which the lottery was held was, in any respect, obviously imperfect, so this method was soon rejected and the drawing was conducted the same way as in other countries: the balls were tossed around violently in an open cylinder, like particles in suspension, then catapulted up, one by one, through centrifugal force. The drawings were always held in public places announced beforehand, and anyone could attend who wished to.

A mischievous idea came to my mind, an idea I readily shared with Messing. I asked him if he could influence the outcome of the drawing while sitting in the hall. If that were possible, perhaps he could make the balls turn up to match either his or my ticket! I told Wolf that I didn't consider such a use of his powers fraudulent or perfidious.

"No," Wolf said when I approached him with this suggestion. "I have no power to influence how the balls will be picked, because they are inanimate objects. It's like making a table turn. I can only give telepathic suggestions to a biological equal, in other words, to another human being. It's another matter, however, if the balls are picked by someone who is invited to do so. He needs a fraction of a second to read the number on the ball, while I need to look at him only half as long, and from a distance, to make out which numerical hieroglyphs have lit up inside his brain.

"Or let's take this whimsical variation. In a glass cylinder, you mix forty-nine people instead of numbered balls, and require six of them to come out of the cylinder in a prescribed order. That's another matter. Since each of them knows his number, it would be no trouble at all for me to order those six persons to jump out in the correct order. Neither the lid nor any force pushing them out would be an obstacle, since the first to rush toward the exit would be the one to whom I gave the command. In that case, you and I could make ourselves rich."

Wolf ended his speech with a fiendish laugh. "But with ivory or plastic balls I can't do anything," he continued. "Do you remember the evangelical parable that faith can move mountains? I have the greatest respect for all beliefs, including Christianity. In it I see man's lofty striving to know the unknown. However, the power to move mountains isn't within the power of the ordinary believer, even the most sincere. It's the prerogative of Christ, or of the saints perhaps. In the same way I, who don't consider myself the prophet of telepathy, can't move a mountain, nor attract the necessary ball. I hope I haven't disillusioned you, Tanya? Still, the potential of the human spirit tends to grow, just like athletic records, which are constantly broken.

"But no matter how many centimeters the high jump record mounts from one Olympic game to the next, I don't think that even the most outstanding athlete will ever cross the bar set above five meters. In my opinion, there is a boundary, a barrier, which the human body isn't capable of exceeding.

"The potential of the soul is boundless, but while the spirit is enclosed in its earthly shell, it will always remain something unknown.

"During my trip to Japan, I was captivated not so much by the exoticism, but by the wisdom people saw in the most ordinary things. For instance, what kind of intellectual food for thought can a public park provide? Well, there is beauty in the design: whimsical flower beds, well-tended sculptures, cascading fountains. But this is all superficial to our search for meaning and mystery in life. Strolling through such a garden, you may be moved by its beauty, but you won't sink into a state of deep meditation. The Japanese have managed to make a park a dwelling for thought, and it is rightfully called a philosophical park. Everything is brilliantly simple. This philosophical park is constructed entirely of stone, including the paths and the fences, even the 'trees.' They are the key ingredient of the park. These 'trees' are really sixteen large stones scattered in a seemingly chaotic fashion throughout the park. Although there *are* sixteen, no matter where you look you see only fifteen, including the one upon which you are standing.

"The sixteenth 'tree,' invisible from any position, represents the lot of man in his striving to know the Truth. He seems to hold it in his hands, but he is unable to embrace its essence. And that, I think, is a good way to describe the occult mysteries."

* * *

When illness strikes a family member or close friend, we protest in powerless indignation. We protest this cruel fate with all our reason and force of will. We always hope that misfortune will bypass those dear to us, especially when we see the unworthy live and prosper. Hopefully, Wolf's philosophy of life prepared him for his own problems.

Wolf Grigoryevich had long suffered pain in his legs, especially when he walked, but he endured it while it was possible. He eventually lost his ability to function normally, and was forced to seek medical help. He turned to his friend, Alexander Alexandrovich Vishnevsky, the Lieutenant General of Medical Services and director of the Institute of Surgery in Moscow. So, in May 1969, Messing spent two weeks at the clinic for treatment. Vishnevsky correctly diagnosed the problem without performing any complicated tests. Wolf was suffering from obliterating endarteritis of both lower extremities, and the surgeon ordered his hospitalization at the institute.

On my first visit to the hospital, I found Messing dispirited by the diagnosis. His doctor prescribed anodynes and forbade him to smoke ever again. He refused to take that last proposal seriously, even though tobacco was his worst enemy under the circumstances. Since I was not allowed to see him at first, Alexander Alexandrovich invited me to wait in his office until Messing's treatment was finished. I sat in a comfortable chair facing the window. The desk in the tiny office was cluttered with case histories, a blood pressure gauge, a stethoscope, and an unfinished breakfast. I was looking idly around when behind me someone said quite loudly and distinctly, "Fool!"

I was dumbfounded; I was sure I was alone in the room. I looked around, but besides some white gowns hanging from a coatrack I could see nothing in the dark corner of the office. So I went back to examining the autographed pictures on the wall, and the shelves filled with books and gifts from patients and various organizations.

Several minutes passed when I again heard that same voice. "Fool!" it shouted. Determined to find the source of the voice, I walked to the dark corner of the room; it took awhile for my eyes to adjust to the darkness. There sat a high round cage, with a black and gray bird about the size of a large parrot inside. But this was an Indian mynah — part of the blackbird family — which is noted for its extraordinary ability to beautifully imitate the human language (in this case Russian).

Glad that I wasn't suffering auditory hallucinations, I said, "And who are you, clever fellow?"

The bird answered matter of factly, "I'm Serezha, I'm good! I'm Serezha, I'm a good boy!" I told the garrulous little boaster that I was very glad, but Serezha didn't listen and poured forth his own talk.

"Patients, return to your wards, to your wards, to your wards..."

Either he was unable to stop, or simply didn't want to. Finally, the master of the bird and the institute walked in.

"What, Serezha, have you already praised yourself?" he asked when he saw me by the cage. "Did you tell Tatyana that you're very clever?"

Serezha grew confused and didn't reply. He hopped from one foot to the other, and finally settled comfortably on his little perch.

Alexander Alexandrovich offered me a seat beside his desk and told me that things were going poorly with Wolf. There was poor circulation in his lower extremities; his blood vessels were covered with sclerotic plates. The surgeon was employing a conservative treatment to relieve and halt the process, but he feared that Wolf's heavy smoking would cause the illness to progress to gangrene, possibly in both legs. In this case, the legs would have to be amputated.

"Wolf Grigoryevich has promised to quit smoking," Professor Vishnevsky said, "but he still hasn't carried it out. I, old fool that I am, believe him every time and . . ."

The physician struck his forehead in frustration, and Serezha interrupted his sentence. "Fool, old fool!" The audacious bird then burst out with a string of obscenities.

Not even a drunkard would carry on in such a way in the presence of a lady! Then I realized the bird was mimicking its master, and it was the professor who was truly guilty. He cursed violently even while performing surgery. Secure in his cage in the professor's office, Serezha had mastered this special language very quickly and willingly employed it. Dr. Vishnevsky was embarrassed, but, unfortunately, it was too late. The pupil had surpassed his teacher.

Vishnevsky told me this talking wonder was a gift brought from India by Uri Gagarin, the first cosmonaut. While we conversed Serezha announced categorically, "Patients, return to your wards. Time for bed!" He wouldn't stop, so we decided to leave the office. It was simply impossible to continue in the bird's presence.

I thereupon went to see Wolf in the ward, eager to tell him about the bird and his habits. Wolf merely smiled and said, "I've also been classed among the fools. Who knows, maybe Serezha is right? Look how many years I've lived among the Russians, and I still haven't mastered their language. Serezha is more capable. And, despite his indecent behavior, people put up with him, and even love him. He should be envied!"

Wolf was hardly a fool, and he didn't lose his legs. But this hospitalization was only the beginning of the medical problems that would eventually end his life.

17

Practical Applications of the Sixth Sense

Like a musician who gets rusty if he doesn't touch his instrument for a long time, so a medical student can't afford to take a lengthy pause from his work. The situation is even more complicated in medicine. The technical equipment we rely upon is constantly evolving, new procedures are perpetually developed, and new drugs come on the market. It is nearly impossible to keep up with it all. My serious illness kept me away from work for seven whole years! I could not work with patients in a clinic, and I was no longer up to the enormous amount of work required of a traveling photojournalist. My sons took a lot of my time, too. I did return to medicine after all, but my work was purely administrative.

I began work at the Bakulev Institute of Heart and Vascular Surgery of the Academy of Sciences. From time to time, the "spirit" of Wolf Messing hovered within the walls of the institute, since he was invisibly involved in the correct diagnosis and outcome of several cases treated there.

When I arrived at work one day, I learned that a seriously ill patient had been admitted during the night. He was an important patient besides, and a group of medical luminaries gathered in conference that morning. A cavalcade of black limousines that accompanied the patient's ambulance lined the front of the hospital. Our charge turned out to be Lieutenant-General Zhukovsky, air force commander of the Byelorussian military district. He was an old friend of Messing's, and he had suffered a severe heart attack which caused an opening in the septum. No one doubted the coronary's fatal outcome. No one had ever before performed an operation for this condition, not at our institute or at any other clinic in the world.

Only the institute's director, Professor Vladimir Burakovsky, had the right to perform an operation on such a gravely ill patient, but he was apprehensive that such an operation would only hasten the patient's death. Yet, to take *no* measures to help Zhukovsky would be just as bad. It was an obviously ticklish situation. Only after an order came from a most unlikely source did the director make his final decision.

During those anxious minutes, my secretary told me Messing had called wanting me to call him back immediately.

"Taibele, tell your boss to begin the operation immediately," he said. "Zhukovsky is my friend and I advise you not to lose one second!"

I told him of Burakovsky's indecision, but Messing interrupted me: "Everything will turn out all right; he'll recover. And your boss will be recommended for an award. Tell him that."

Seeing no other way to resolve the situation, Burakovsky finally agreed to undertake the operation, hoping for a miracle to save the patient's life. The long operation was completed and the first critical days passed without incident. Zhukovsky was transferred to the Burdenko clinic for further observation. It was an amazing recovery for a man for whom, a short while earlier, funeral wreaths could have been ordered. If Messing hadn't called in the nick of time, the delay in surgery would have been tragic. Professor Burakovsky was awarded the title of Corresponding Member of the Academy of Medical Sciences, and decorated for the successful operation — the first of its kind ever performed in the USSR .

I'm certain that Wolf Messing never analyzed his premonitions or other psychic impressions; they came to him as complete information. When I later asked him whether he felt he was taking a risk in urging Professor Burakovskv to operate on Zhukovsky, Messing was typically nonchalant.

"I didn't even think about that," he explained. "The chain of associations — operation … Zhukovsky … life — simply arose in my consciousness. And that's all."

That didn't explain very much to me. An understanding of Messing's power remained beyond my grasp.

Since we were close friends, I didn't feel awkward asking Wolf Grigoryevich if there were any unsuccessful situations where he had failed to avert a tragic fate. Wolf of course understood that I wasn't referring to the unavoidable errors he made during his stage performances, but to more personal failures. Messing tossed his head nervously. He reached for a cigarette, even though a freshly lit one lay in the ash tray. After inhaling deeply several times, he answered.

"People really *do* influence each other," he began. "What are you doing, reading my thoughts? I've been wanting to tell you about a particular incident for a long time, but never found a pretext…"

"And now you've brought it up yourself. No, I've never made any gross errors," he responded. "I'm including all the individual tasks that have been given to me or those in which I took the initiative, especially life or death cases. I'm sure you remember the case with Mstislav Keldysh, president of the Academy of Sciences. He was brought to your institute even though they knew that none of your celebrated physicians would perform an operation on him. A decision had been made at a high governmental level to invite a brigade of American physicians, headed by the famous Michael DeBakey, to consult on the case. You already know the result.* As far as concerns life's race to the

---

* In 1972, Keldysh needed some sort of vascular surgery, and the Soviet Union invited Dr. Michael DeBakey to perform it, an unprecedented move. The precise nature of the surgery was not revealed at that time, but it was successful — *editor's note.*

finish line, I will be the first to cross the ribbon … and some instructions concerning my funeral will be issued by Keldysh. You will see for yourself."

I listened in horror to this cryptic dialogue, and for the first time I wanted Wolf Grigoryevich to stop the conversation. He continued calmly.

"Let's put aside these mournful recriminations and get back to the subject. I shall never forgive myself for my indecisiveness regarding a tragedy with which you are well familiar. The tragic premonition came to me spontaneously, even though there was no clear image of catastrophe. "I awoke at the crack of dawn on that morning in April 1967, and decided to take a walk about Moscow's still sleeping streets. The newspapers were already on sale at the newsstands, and I bought several different morning editions. Front-page headlines concerned the successful launch of the space ship "Soyus 1," and there were pictures of the cosmonaut, Vladimir Komarov. The forty-year-old Komarov was rather short, with thin, narrow lips and thick eyebrows. The inside pages included articles on the flight, biographies of Komarov, and pictures taken of him at Red Square and in the Kremlin just before the launch. I looked at these photographs, trying hard to psychically read his facial features. With lightning speed the impression 'he will not return' flashed through my mind. I felt a shiver run down my spine, and, for an instant, the impression seemed ridiculous. But the nagging thought wouldn't leave me alone. I saw no concrete vision of catastrophe, and I assumed the persistent phrase was simply left over from some other impression.

"I tried to expel all thoughts of the launch. But while I was caring breakfast, the phrase flared up three times, like a signal inside my head: he will not return … he will not return … he will not return.

"I couldn't relax since I didn't clearly understand the meaning of the signal. Putting aside my half-finished tea, I lay down on the sofa to concentrate. But, even then, no specific pictures came through.

"Next I began to meditate in an attempt to put everything concerning the impression in its proper place. That was my first and major mistake! For in such cases, trying to reason through an impression is more of an obstacle than anything else. I should have simply accepted the signal unconditionally and tried to take some measures to change fate ... although even today I am far from sure the catastrophe could have been averted. Anyway, decisions regarding our space programs belong to our political leaders. They would scarcely have listened to my mystical prognostications.

"My reasoning followed these lines: Why won't he return? The spaceship, launched into a circular orbit around the earth, wouldn't fly off into the fathomless expanse of space. Even if the rocket burned up upon re-entry, the capsule containing the cosmonaut's body, would certainly return to earth. So he *would* return. I certainly didn't believe that he'd be intercepted by alien space craft!

"This line of thinking was so confusing, I became indecisive. Clairvoyance *is* illogical; trying to logically sort out the impressions that arise from it is senseless.

"I didn't have to wait long for a solution to the mystery. Within a few days, it was officially announced that Vladimir Komarov had died on April 24, 1967, while returning from orbit. Despite my foreknowledge of the event, I was saddened by the news."

To be sure, "logic" played a small role in Messing's clairvoyance and precognitive powers. His procedures were the antithesis of the methodology Sherlock Holmes would use. Deduction and analysis played no part when he solved crimes or otherwise helped the police.

In 1928 or 1929 while performing in Paris, Wolf was invited to a small provincial town to solve the poisoning death of a wealthy widow. The prefect could offer Messing no leads; no clues had yet been uncovered. Accompanied by two detectives, Messing went to the victim's villa. Her son, a young man of eighteen or twenty, small of stature, but very good-looking, acted as his guide. Passing from one room to the next, giving them but a cursory glance, Messing stopped suddenly at an old painting in a room adjacent to the bedroom. It was a portrait of the murdered woman — an aristocratic lady in a wedding dress. After pondering the painting for some time, he turned to the young man.

"Kindly surrender the key hanging behind the portrait to the police," he said. "You opened the safe with it after you poisoned your mother."

Within the hour the youth gave his testimony to the prefect.

A year later, back home in Poland, a grieving family asked Messing to locate a young man from Torun who was missing. Messing was familiar with the circumstances, and he immediately volunteered to go to Torun. He spent two days in the home of the distressed family. On the third day, while in a near-cataleptic trance, he told the parents: "Your Yuzef is dead. The body is in the river right behind the bridge, and the head is in a public lavatory." Then he named the street. However, he could not get a clear "picture" of the murderer.

As far as I know, Wolf never used his powers for purely political purposes, even though his detractors constantly spread such rumors. But he often talked about one case he was proud of, involving German espionage during World War II.

A suspicious-looking man was arrested in 1944 near Novgorod. Tall, blond, broad-shouldered, and wearing horn-rimmed glasses, he looked stereotypically German, and immediately admitted that he was indeed German. The security officers were sure that he was an important member of Germany's intelligence service, but they had no proof. Realizing that he was doomed, the German stubbornly insisted on his innocence. The security force tortured him and even arranged a mock execution to frighten him into confessing, but nothing worked. He was one of those rare people who can withstand great pain without cracking under it. The security people didn't want to shoot him; they were convinced of his connection to a whole espionage network.

The following was the German prisoner's version of his presence in the Soviet Union: He found himself on a Russian battlefield after suffering a severe contusion and made it to the nearest village, which turned out to be totally abandoned. He spent three months hiding in a barn, burned his uniform, and put on some peasant clothing that he had discovered in a storeroom. He subsisted on food that had been left in the village cellars, and sometimes shot wild game with the pistol he kept for that purpose. He didn't know a single word of Russian.

This last claim sparked the officers' suspicions. They suspected that he really did know the language and could speak it fluently, but he hadn't given himself away during the entire four weeks of his confinement.

At that point in the investigation they turned to Messing. They wanted to know if the prisoner understood the conversations conducted in his presence in Russian. Wolf was asked to attend one or two of the interrogations in the guise of a high-ranking official (though he dressed in civilian clothes). He did not, however, take any part in the conversation itself.

Within a half hour of the first session, during which they asked him simple questions such as his name and date and place of birth, Messing telepathically determined that the prisoner was mentally translating everything from Russian into German when spoken to by the interpreter. Messing knew that the prisoner was a seasoned spy. But how could his impression be proved? Within twenty-five minutes, Wolf came up with a brilliant plan, which he proceeded to execute that very day and which he later looked back on with much pride. His plan was so cogent that the spy fell quickly into the trap.

A cross-examination in Russian was begun by the chief investigator in the presence of a secretary. Unlike the chief investigator, Messing — befitting the role he was playing as a Soviet official — remained completely silent. He was self-controlled and calm, which is rare for someone who is carrying out such high-level orders. The suspect looked searchingly toward Messing the whole time, as if pleading for sympathy.

When the routine questioning was completed, Messing tapped his finger on the folder he carried with him and said in perfect German, "Yes, I am now totally convinced that you are not guilty of anything."

Then he got up from his chair, saying in the same breath, but in Russian, "That's all. You are free to go."

The prisoner jumped up instantly, only to realize the fatal mistake he'd made. He tried to sit back down, but it was already too late.

When Wolf first told me this story, I asked, "So there are practically no criminal cases — even the most complicated — which must necessarily remain unsolved? Wouldn't it be sufficient for each government to retain a telepath or two to help with security and criminal investigations? That way there would be neither unjust sentences nor unsolved cases."

"No, not so!" Wolf said resolutely. "Abilities such as mine can't serve as a panacea for crime. Every just and democratic judgment must be guided by fact.

"That incident with the fascist intelligence officer was special and can't serve as an example for law enforcement agencies in general. I agreed to take part in the investigation only because the circumstances called for special measures.

"It's debatable whether a parapsychologist or telepath should help in criminal investigations or trials. The problem is similar to knowing whether to perform organ transplant operations if the donor is only *close* to death. The issue had been widely discussed in medical circles years before Dr. Christian Barnard performed the first heart transplant in South Africa. The issue wasn't about the practical side of the matter, but the tricky moral and ethical problems involved. How can you guarantee that the donor, perhaps suffering the aftereffects of an accident, is in a truly hopeless state? Where do we stop helping one person to save the life of another?

Nobody can rightfully judge unless the donor is truly dead.

"No telepath working with a criminal case can be substituted for a proper investigation and trial. He can be employed in a limited way to find evidence, but little more. That's the role I played in some sensational European trials.

"An opinion unfortunately shared by many jurists is that every criminal leaves behind some clue, however minute, of his presence. In my opinion, this point of view is wrong.

"A great many crimes, especially those committed by professional criminals, are executed without a trace. If any clues are left behind, time and the elements erase them. Such crimes are extremely difficult to solve, and it's nearly impossible to determine the guilt of any suspects taken into custody. Persistent and painstaking investigatory work must be undertaken in such cases; the impressions of a clairvoyant can only be used as guides to the investigator. In no case can they serve to build an accusation. Let me give you an example.

"In 1951, the ancient town of Kazan on the Volga was filled with rumors concerning the mysterious murder of a nineteen-year-old girl. It was a classic case of a crime without a clue. She was thrown from a bridge in the middle of the night. The girl, of slight build, wouldn't have been hard to lift. Perhaps someone, in a moment of mock tenderness, hurled her deftly over the bridge railing.

"Her former boyfriend, who was as thin and pale as the drowned girl, was arrested many months later, even though there were no grounds for suspicion. Many witnesses testified at his trial that he hadn't seen the victim for two years. But when they were dating, they were seen together on the bridge quite often, and the accusations against the youth were all based on this fact. The fellow was crushed, possibly grieved over the death of his former love and the stress of the trial. He said nothing intelligible in his defense, merely repeating over and over the same sentence: 'It wasn't me.'"

Luckily, Wolf Messing was in Kazan during the trial, which had lasted more than a week — a lengthy period for a small-town trial. Wolf learned of the controversial trial from a hotel maid, a habitué of spicy open trial proceedings. He decided to attend the trial when he had some time to spare.

By the morning recess, Wolf knew the defendant was innocent. At the same time, Messing latched onto someone else's nervous ruminations — perhaps the perpetrator's last recollections before throwing his victim into the river. At the beginning of the trial, Wolf sat tranquilly. But later, he began to feel bouts of nervousness, because he felt the murderer's own impulses welling up inside of him.

Wolf returned to the hotel by foot, and while walking he focused inward on his impressions. He knew that many murderers are drawn again and again, as though by a magnet, to the place of their crimes; many such cases are recorded in the annals of criminal justice. But Wolf believed that, in the present case, the bridge really wasn't important, but the river below. In any event, the water movement deprived the scene of "concreteness," and he didn't think the criminal would return to it. He also believed that his initial impression in the courtroom had come directly from the murderer.

The task now remained for Wolf to visualize the murderer during the next day's session. He intuitively felt the man would show up at every session.

Wolf was among the first to enter the courtroom before the proceedings the next day, so that he could examine everyone as they came in. Two young boys, apparently friends of the defendant, rushed into the courtroom first. One of them was dressed in sports clothes and the other in a well-worn gray suit. Behind them followed a quiet middle-aged woman and a somewhat older man. They were the parents of the defendant. Gradually the hall was filled to the limit with spectators. Unfortunately, Wolf wasn't able to finger the murderer. But when the trial began, similar impressions to those he'd received the previous day burst into his mind. Now he merely had to "focus in" on the source.

Messing sat in the courtroom for about ten minutes with his eyes closed, as if lost in a trance. Then he looked to his left, toward the last seat on the fifth row aisle from the defendant's bench. Seated there was a man in his midtwenties holding a rolled up copy of the magazine *Ogonyok*. *This* was the person sending the nervous impulses, Wolf realized. The psychic then sent the man a telepathic instruction: "Rise, tell them you're the murderer!"

The young man began to fidget in his seat even more noticeably. He pulled out a pack of cigarettes, put them back, and with feigned interest examined the pictures in the paper. Then he rolled up the paper once again. Fear seemed to take hold of him so that he couldn't bring himself to do anything more.

Messing was satisfied as to the source of his impressions. The person's extreme nervousness would help the psychic shatter him. But how? Wolf decided that some kind of graphic jolt was necessary.

When the first recess was announced, the young man straightened out the newspaper and placed it on his seat to signal that it was occupied. During the interval Wolf knocked at the door of the court office and, posing as the new building steward, asked the secretary for a piece of white paper and a red pencil. He explained that he wanted to place a sign in the smoking room, because some people were confusing it with the exit. He wrote out in large letters: NO EXIT ...

Unlike most such signs, this one had those suggestive three dots, carefully added by Messing.

When the session resumed, Wolf ignored the testimony of the participants, and bombarded the young man with the mental command: Rise! Tell them you're the murderer!

During the second recess, Wolf waited until he was alone in the courtroom. He then slipped the sign underneath the newspaper the young man left behind on his seat.

Messing left to smoke his cigarette, but didn't return to the courtroom. He didn't want to see the inevitable painful confession. When the session resumed, he waited by a half-opened door. He didn't have to wait long. Soon the entire room shook with the heartrending cry, "I'm the one! I killed her!"

Messing wasn't interested in the rest. Satisfied with his good deed, he walked home.

18

The Crisis Continues

People dread the coming of fall with its lingering rain, dank fog, and early twilight. Spring, on the other hand, brings cheerfulness and hope. But, for several years, I had come to anticipate April's flowers with ever-growing anxiety. Every year, with the return of the greenery and warmth, Wolf entered the hospital. In early spring, 1972, it was once again time for his yearly examination and treatment at Vishnevsky's clinic. A tall, completely modern and comfortable building was added to the old. Wolf had a private room. On my first visit he quipped that he felt he was resting in a sanatorium, not a hospital. But I knew the price he paid for this outwardly cheerful pose. The chronic pains in his legs were getting worse, forcing him to stoop over. His bony, dangling arms and tousled head added to his vulnerable appearance. He showed no signs of mental feebleness, and maintained the demeanor of a child, taking enthusiastic joy in everything around him. He seemed to me the same Wolf Messing I knew twenty years ago.

I wasn't able to spend much time with him during my first visit; I was in a rush to get to the institute. I needed to pick up plasma from a blood transfusion station. I returned two days later, and Wolf was in the courtyard wearing an Eastern-style robe instead of a hospital gown. This was a privilege granted more distinguished patients. He was indescribably happy to see me.

It was May, and the sun was hot in the courtyard. We sat down on a bench by an old maple tree to talk. I handed Wolf some goodies not to be found on the hospital menu: an early spring vegetable and berry assortment from the Caucasus, a bag of large strawberries, and some fresh tomatoes.

Messing finished the strawberries on the spot, saving the tomatoes for dinner.

He suggested an excursion through the courtyard's secluded corners and front garden.

"Here I lose myself in thought about the transience of our lives," Wolf said as he led me to a memorial erected in honor of Alexander Vasilievich Vishnevsky, Alexander Alexandrovich's father. "You never know what will come into your head when you stand next to this old sage … with a scalpel on his mind," Wolf added. The memorial depicted Alexander Vishnevsky in full hospital attire, but it was made in dark gray granite. He did resemble a sage, his pose reminiscent of Rodin's "The Thinker."

Next we headed toward the hospital's old building, and I could easily guess where Messing was dragging me.

Beside an open window, Dr. Vishnevsky's pet bird Serezha perched royally on a bar in his cage. Messing liked to have long talks with him, but Serezha was now in a cage far removed from the clinic's staff and residents. The bird was being punished for abusing his linguistic talents with profanity while a high-ranking foreign delegation of medical students paid a surprise visit. Two of the delegates commanded a fair knowledge of Russian and were suitably shocked.

Wolf Grigoryevich attempted a heart-to-heart talk but Serezha wasn't in the mood to reciprocate. Being removed from his own cozy cage was clearly an insult, and he showered Messing with saliva in parting.

"That's something new in his repertoire," Messing grumbled, wiping his robe.

Dr. Vishnevsky soon lifted the bird's punishment, and the mynah was returned to his old cage in his master's office. Messing offered the physician three thousand rubles for the lively bird, but Vishnevsky, very attached to the bird, refused to give him up.

Messing was burdened by mundane problems. He shared a oneroom apartment with a housekeeper, hired in 1972 when Iraida Mikhailovna died. It wasn't in character for Messing to ask the government for more tolerable living quarters, but, luckily, a woman from the Ministry of Culture, well-disposed toward Wolf, came to his assistance. She arranged for him to use his own money to rent a two-room apartment on Herzen Street in a house built for ministry workers. His apartment was on the thirteenth floor.

"And what do you think of the 'devil's dozen?'"I asked Wolf.

"Devils are my hobby! I get along great with them,"he joked.

There were fewer and fewer lighthearted moments in Messing's life. The following spring saw another return to the hospital, where he now spent much of his time. His walks had shortened, so Wolf had brought more books than usual — books he had been too busy to read earlier.

"If only the people who gave them to me knew that I've never opened them,"Wolf said as he held up two large volumes, both autographed by their authors. Dr. A. A. Vishnevsky's *A Surgeon's Diary* contained the following inscription: "To Wolf Grigoryevich Messing in fond memory from the author — A. Vishnevsky. March 27, 1969."

As is well known in the Soviet Union, Dr. Vishnevsky contributed enormously to the fight against the epidemics that raged in the front lines during World War II. He also performed emergency surgery on the battlefields. His book was therefore published with an introduction by the outstanding military commander, Marshal G. Zhukov.

The second book, *Thoughts and the Heart*, was written by Nikolai Amosov, a well-known surgeon and essayist. His book was inscribed with more moving words: "To Wolf Grigoryevich Messing as a sign of wonderment and admiration of a miracle — Amosov, December 25, 1965."

Iraida had read Messing extracts from these books, but he never found time to pick them up himself. He decided to now fill in the gaps. They were just what he needed: good, wise books about the strength of the human spirit and transience of the body.

"You see," he said while pointing to the books, "I cannot complain about the absence of friends. They visit me both at home and here. But I shall die totally alone …"

By the end of the summer of 1974, however, the crisis seemed to have passed. Wolf was clearly on the road to recovery, but he was released with strict instructions to completely rest at home.

Exhausted by the situation, I left for Gagry on the seashore at the beginning of October to vacation. Suntanned and feeling stronger, I returned to Moscow late October thirtieth. The next day I awoke to the frantic ringing of the telephone. "Lord, another workday!" I thought to myself. But it wasn't work calling; it was a physician from the institute who said, "Your friend Wolf Grigoryevich is here. He's in very bad shape and will have to undergo a serious operation to replace part of the iliac arteries and abdominal aorta."

I knew what the obstruction of blood to the lower extremities meant, especially for someone in his seventies like Wolf Messing. I wasn't panic-stricken, however; he was in our institute where everyone knew of my friendship with him, and that guaranteed him sensitive and attentive care. Since Wolf was already in surgery, I didn't think it necessary to go to the institute immediately. I kept in constant touch with the on-duty physician in the recovery section in case complications resulted.

I discovered that Wolf performed in the Trans-Carpathian Mountains during my visit to Gagry. Each performance for two years past had been an enormous effort for him. Wolf cut short his last stage appearance because of a terrible pain that doubled him over, and he and his manager took the first flight back to Moscow. Valentina Iosifovna told me that, while helping Wolf to the ambulance, the psychic stopped and glanced sorrowfully at his house. "I'll never see it again," he said. Professor Burakovsky, the institute's director, advised Wolf to get to the hospital immediately.

Unlike the many other times he was hospitalized, he seemed nervous and devoid of his usual stoicism. Was his remark some sort of grave premonition? Was he grieved that no one ever petitioned the Soviet government to fulfill his long-standing request — that the famous Michael DeBakey be brought to the USSR to operate on him? In 1972, Dr. DeBakey successfully performed the same operation Wolf required on M. Keldysh, the president of the Soviet Union's Academy of Sciences. Wolf had even offered to pay all of Dr. DeBakey's expenses himself, regardless of the cost. Despite this setback, it was fortunate for Wolf that my friend Anatoly Vladimirovich Pokrovsky was to perform the operation.

The day following the operation, I went tearing to the resuscitation section to find out how Wolf was faring, but I was suffering from a cold and wasn't allowed to enter. I threw on a white gown, fastened a mask over my face, and observed the sad proceedings through the glass window. Messing was breathing with the help of a respirator, but, amazingly enough, he was signaling with his hands that he wanted to smoke! Even in such a critical condition, Wolf could think of nothing but his cigarettes. The attending physician recognized me and nodded, holding up his thumb to signal that all was well.

Wolf's legs were a normal color, a good sign because, in such cases, the skin often turns blue and then gangrenous. The danger had passed once more. As far as I was concerned, he'd get that poisonous tobacco over my dead body!

It was important for Wolf to recover without complications. Relaxed vigilance after successful surgery often spoils everything. But what right did I have to give advice? Dr. Pokrovsky had taken personal responsibility and the cards were in his hands. I exchanged a few words with Wolf's manager, who came to the institute when the crisis began; we agreed to share any news we heard.

Expressing hopeful thoughts, we left for home.

I wasn't feeling too well myself that evening, and I woke up the next morning with a cough that grew progressively worse. After swallowing a few spoon fills of warm milk with honey, I rushed to the phone to find out how Wolf was doing. The physician on duty reported that Messing had suffered pulmonary collapse, but the doctors hoped to pull him through.

By that afternoon the worsening situation became critical. Messing's kidneys had ceased to function, threatening to poison his entire system. My only consolation was that his pulse was even and his sleep reasonably tranquil.

Rumors of Wolf's serious illness soon spread throughout Moscow, and his condition caused his friends growing alarm. Those who knew us both didn't stand on ceremony, and I was called to the telephone several times a day and at all hours. I spent that entire period between October 31 and November 8 by a telephone. I felt like an international operator, but I never got a change of shift! During the rare moments the telephone was silent, I called the institute always with the same question: How is Wolf Messing?

Eight days of this tension and anxiety slipped by. On the evening of November 8, crowds celebrated the last day of the October holidays; I, however, was troubled and depressed. At ten o'clock I again called the physician on duty but there was no comfort. Messing was still critical; his kidneys were still not functioning.

The enormous strain of those days exacerbated my own illness; I now had pneumonia. I fell into a deep sleep and awoke at six-thirty the next morning with no recollection of going to bed. I looked with alarm at the telephone sitting so silently on the table. At eight-thirty it finally rang.

It was Alexander Davydovich, head of the section in which Messing was hospitalized, with bad news: Wolf died at eleven o'clock the previous night. Knowing that I was ill, he decided to withhold the information until morning.

It was up to me to relate the tragic news to Wolf's other friends. I immediately called Valentina Ivanovskaya, and had just hung up the receiver when my mind was pierced like lightning with the thought: his brain! Wolf Messing's brain! It must be preserved.

I had heard long before how Wolf Messing's brain had been valued at one million dollars. What blasphemy, I thought. Who would buy such a property, and who would be the seller? If his brain could contribute something to science, then it belonged to everyone. No one could rightfully claim exclusive ownership. Chopin's heart is buried in Poland, but his music belongs to everyone.

Time was flying by. At any moment, a surgeon could perform a trepanation of Wolf's skull, a procedure so gruesome that it causes the hair on the heads of fledgling medical students to stand on end. (Each section of the brain is placed in the deceased person's stomach upon examination.) I immediately dialed the home number of Professor Pokrovsky and expressed my apprehensions. He replied that he was on leave from work, and the postmortem examination had been entrusted to Professor Leonid Krymsky. He assured me Krymsky could be relied upon. I tried to call Professor Krymsky, but his number had recently been changed. Some woman answered my call and thoroughly questioned me before finally explaining how I could get in touch with him. Who was I? Why was I calling? When I finally reached his home, I learned that he'd already left for the clinic to perform the postmortem.

I was too late! My nerves were at the breaking point. If only I could get to the institute in time!

My son, Sasha, was the only on-duty doctor at the dermatology-venereal hospital that day, so there was little chance of getting him away even for thirty minutes. But to call tor a taxi on a Sunday was a waste of time. I decided to talk Sasha into violating his duties in order to drive me to the hospital, even while the postmortem was being performed, but he refused because of my own medical condition.

I told him sternly, "Alexander, this is not a conversation between mother and son. You know our motto: no joking in serious matters!" (I really wanted to say, "This isn't just Wolf's friend speaking; this is a friend of *Messing*!") "This is something more important than my health," I continued. "Get into the car and follow me!"

Within fifteen minutes I was flying into Professor Krymsky's office. I immediately began to explain.

"We understand the situation," the professor replied, pointing with a friendly gesture to an armchair nearby. "Even if a thorough investigation proves unimpressive for science, we must in any event preserve his brain, if only as a symbolic gesture. I have friends at the Institute of Brain Research, and I promise they will take care of this matter."

I heaved a sigh of relief and almost collapsed in the chair. My nerves seemed to cave in, and, for the first time since Wolf's death, I got a lump in my throat.

The painful moment was interrupted by a knock at the door. It was Wolf's manager, there at my request. I introduced them but the professor soon left us together in the office while he and Sasha attended to the postmortem.

Valentina had come, and we waited impatiently for their return. Sasha came back alone, in a hurry to return to his own hospital. He told me that Pokrovsky's operation had been brilliantly executed. The psychic's death was most probably due to mistakes made during the postoperative period, due to a lack of vigilance on the part of the staff. The director had, unfortunately, been on vacation when the operation took place, and the remaining personnel didn't have the necessary control.

Unfortunately, this is characteristic of medical care in the USSR, especially when surgery is involved. The brilliant successes of great physicians are often reduced to zero by insufficient nursing care, malnutrition, and shortages of medications or instruments.

Wolf had evidently foreseen the situation, which is why he had offered to pay to bring Dr. DeBakey and his team of assistants from the United States for the operation. The high success rate of Dr. DeBakey's operations was truly impressive. It is a tragedy that Messing's request was left unfulfilled.

As for his brain? It was in a sclerotic condition, but there was no visible pathological deterioration. Its weight was standard. In a word , the psychic's brain was perfectly normal.

I had experienced a vague presentiment of what we would find. Messing's brain would have been of interest to science only if it revealed some evidence of his power as a telepath, but there was little chance this would happen. Research on parapsychological phenomena is still in its infancy. We don't have the necessary instruments to detect such evidence, nor are scientists sensitive or qualified enough to know what to look for.

Later, Sasha and I went to Wolf's apartment to begin the prefuneral arrangements.

The only notice announcing Wolf Messing's death appeared in *Evening Moscow* on November 14, six days after his passing. The announcement was probably delayed so as not to cloud the celebrations commemorating the anniversary of the Russian Revolution. The death date was correctly given, but the notice didn't mention the funeral. Most readers probably thought it had already taken place. Few people besides his close friends knew when or where the funeral was to take place. At least the Ministry of Culture gave instructions that Messing's casket be placed in the Central House for Workers in the Arts (TsDRI) for a memorial service.

Valentina lvanovskaya, my son Sasha, a few of Messing's friends, and I went to the morgue. Messing's coffin was mounted on a modest replica of a gun carriage of the sort that carries the remains of prominent military commanders or statesmen.

Aleksei, one of Wolf's friends, pulled a small pair of scissors from his pocket and snipped a small lock of curly gray hair from

Messing's temple. He placed it carefully in an envelope inside an address book. Even though he had been raised in an intellectual Russian family, they regarded the psychic, who had done many good deeds for them, as a saint.

We maintained our sad watch until an official from the Moscow City Council Department of Culture arrived. We decided to close the coffin and attend the memorial service.

When we arrived at October Square, our car was stopped by a traffic inspection officer who announced that Dmitrov Street would be closed for two hours. When we asked why the officer replied, "You mean you don't know? Today Wolf Messing is to be buried, and the procession will pass along this highway."

"We're very touched by the concern of the police," I replied with sad irony, "but Messing's body is in our car. We're going to TsDRI. We'll be coming back through here this afternoon."

A crowd had already formed at the entrance. The police were maintaining order; there was one policeman for every two mourners! No one was openly crying, although some of the middle-aged women carried tear-soaked handkerchiefs. There would have been a larger turnout had the authorities announced the funeral date on time! Possibly they feared a pilgrimage of students, among whom Messing was enormously popular, or a cortege of religious believers who considered Messing holy. This latter group were considered undesirable participants, since nothing would ever shake their conviction that Messing's abilities were gifts from heaven. In fact, when the coffin was carried through the hall, a middle-aged woman said, "A holy man has departed."

I was standing with the honor guard when Uri Nikulin, a famous clown and a personal favorite of Wolf's, entered the hall. Silently and somehow very bashfully, he tiptoed to the coffin as if committing some offense. He positioned himself next to me. Casting a cursory glance at him, I noticed that there were still traces of makeup on his face. He was filming a motion picture and had interrupted his work to offer his last respects.

Both acquaintances and strangers alike placed bouquets or wreaths by the coffin, standing by for a moment in silence.

Finally, the time came for the burial. The crowd outside had increased by a hundred people, but the police forbade anyone entrance into the hall.

In the Soviet Union, by law, each grave must be registered and assigned to a close relative, guardian, or friend empowered to act for the deceased. This person has the right to choose the place and manner of burial, and to secure a guarantee from the cemetery's administration for the proper maintenance of the grave site. Since I was the only person close to him at the time of his death, I was granted this honor. I wanted to see Wolf buried at the Vostryakov cemetery, beside his wife, Aida Mikhailovna. At one-thirty we arrived at this melancholy place. I needn't describe the emotional service that followed. We then returned to the TsDRI for a traditional funeral repast. The tables were moved into a single row, not to save space, but in accordance with an old Russian tradition that would have people seated closely together, as if members of a large family. And, in fact, we *were* a family, all thirty of us.

A gloomy-looking fellow from the Ministry of Arts started the eulogies following that old formula: speak only good things about the dead or nothing at all. He spent most of his time listing Messing's services to society, including the donation of the fighter planes and his patronage of an orphanage. But, for some reason, he forgot to mention how Wolf had attracted an audience of a million people, bringing the government incalculable profit. Nor did he propose that any funds be set aside for parapsychological research. Even in death, Wolf's life work was relegated to the achievements of a theatrical performer.

But Aleksei, who served Messing faithfully all his life, spoke from his heart with warmth and feeling. Then many others, out of gratitude or admiration, came forward to speak.

I was the last. I was overcome by emotion and my words were uneven, but everyone understood me. We all recalled the happy days and hours we had been fortunate enough to spend with Messing. Proper etiquette precluded my taking notes, but I listened attentively; echoes of these stories have been included in several of this book's essays.

Valentina Iosifovna Ivanovskaya and I were among the last to leave the banquet. Messing's former manager accompanied me to a taxi stand. We parted affectionately, but without words.

Sometimes misfortune doesn't permit us to weaken. This one mobilized my inner resources. I had long ago decided that a book would be the best memorial to Wolf.

19

Nothing Human is Alien

While gathering material for this book and working on it both in Moscow and later in the United States, I drew upon the suggestions of several close friends. Some of these people knew Wolf Messing well, and others were just acquaintances, but both groups gave me kind advice and added considerably to this book. My goal has been to preserve Messing's total image, avoiding gossip and the temptation to present him as a miracle worker. However, opinions about the specific form and content of these memoirs varied considerably among those I consulted. Some wholeheartedly approved my preliminary drafts, while others disliked the way I diluted the manuscript with everyday, mundane details. They felt I cluttered the book with trivia, and suggested I write it more like a best-selling detective novel.

Tormented by doubt, I read about ten books from the "The Lives of Remarkable People," a series published in the USSR. I remained fully convinced that the "gripping novel" approach to Messing's biography would be ill-advised.

Wolf Messing wasn't a Sherlock Holmes. While Messing occasionally played the role of detective, this was certainly not the focus of his life's work. Nor did he share much in common with Arthur Conan Doyle's refined, intellectual hero. Wolf Messing remained a mystery even to me, though I knew him for so many years. But despite the puzzle that was Messing, I wanted to present a multifaceted portrait of him as psychic, husband, friend, animal lover, and human being. I wanted to reduce the mystery he posed to science — to bring him down to earth, so to speak.

I don't think I am compromising Messing by this depiction. He suffered the same problems we all do. He wasn't always even-tempered and obliging, never overcame his addiction to tobacco, and was neither a Puritan nor a libertine. In other words, the ancient saying "I am a human being, and nothing human is alien to me" certainly suited him.

It is even more mysterious that, in such an ordinary mortal shell, such an unknown power was so refined. We like to marvel at geniuses — people fluent in scores of foreign languages, or computer or chess wizards, for example. But at least we can comprehend their powers. They may be entrancing and their powers inaccessible to most of us, but we can understand the basics of their gifts. Yet after witnessing even one of Messing's sessions, I doubt whether anyone could hazard a guess about the principles or power underlying his abilities.

I was crushed by Wolf Messing's death, but I had to overcome my loss; there was important business to see to. First, we had to properly honor his memory. His monument at the Vostryakov Cemetery had to be erected, and, of course, I had to begin this book.

Meanwhile, the state of my health left much to be desired. Pneumonia is no joking matter, especially if complications are not eliminated in time. Fortunately, I was surrounded by the sensitive care of my son Sasha and his fiancée, who took over many of my daily burdens.

But somewhat later, several events characteristic of a low-grade detective novel began to unfold. Valentina Ivanovskaya called to tell me that she had received a summons to appear at the local police station, for a meeting that had to do with Wolf Messing. I received a similar note the next day with more information. We were to witness an inventory taken of Wolf's possessions. I couldn't ignore the notice despite my health, and at the specified time, a car was obligingly sent for me to take me to Wolf's apartment. Two representatives from the First Notorial Office of Moscow, Valentina, and I attended.

The lawyers drew up the official forms and began to methodically inspect the apartment. They opened the ancient, locked, ironbound trunk. At one time it had been filled with Aida Mikhailovna's things, but now it was empty save for some yellowing newspapers, and, underneath them, a belt with two small pockets that I had made for Wolf. The pockets were for important papers and for the three-carat diamond ring that Messing carried as a talisman. If he didn't wear it on his hand, then he either wore it by his breast or carried it in the belt's little pocket. There were some photographs in the trunk as well.

The pocket for the ring turned out to be empty, but bank books showing slightly more than a million predevaluation rubles (not counting ten to fifteen years of interest) were in the other. They also found cash totaling eight hundred rubles.

No will was discovered, so we — his close friends — expressed our wish to use the cash for a memorial. Our petition, however, was to little avail. The lawyers explained that, since Messing had no direct heir, the money would become the property of the state, as if the state weren't already in eternal debt to him for the enormous sums of money Wolf's performances had brought them!

This whole tawdry procedure was finally finished and we signed the statement, relieved to be rid of this burden. But no such luck! In the following days many of Wolf's friends were summoned to the Office of the Public Prosecutor, and I was summoned to the dismally notorious Lubyanka Prison, which certainly didn't bode well for me.

Everyone was asked the same question: What had happened to those jewels Messing had smuggled into the country when escaping from Poland? Where had his famous ring disappeared to? Interestingly, this ring gained a carat every passing day. Within a few days I was called back.

The public prosecutors even conducted a search of Messing's housekeeper, but they didn't find anything belonging to Wolf — his expensive chandelier, old china, or Faberge crystal — in her possession. Nor did they find the many gifts he had received over the years. He had collected the most unexpected things; an exhibit could have been created from the children's toys and folk crafts, pictures and embossed metal, hand-embroidered oriental robes, seashells and coral from Far Eastern sailors he accumulated. Gifts from teachers and schoolchildren, workers, doctors, peasants, craftsmen, and soldiers were all included in his collection. But nothing turned up.

During Messing's last illness and after his death, only his housekeeper had keys to the apartment. Ironically, the officials now needed a Wolf Messing to put the puzzle together. None of Lubyanka's Sherlock Holmeses proved to be telepathic.

The year passed, and gradually I recovered and began work on this book. But thoughts about a memorial for Wolf never left my mind. His plot had only a name plate, as if a nameless wanderer lay there. His friend Aleksei had attached a small photograph. He became actively involved in the cause too, and Valentina wrote a long letter to the Ministry of Culture, reminding them of Messing's services to the Soviet government. We especially emphasized his enormous material contribution to the war effort, which we hoped would influence them more than anything else. Although Wolf undoubtedly made an even greater contribution to science and parapsychology, this legacy awaits proper evaluation. We felt that Messing also deserved to be remembered for his state honors: he had received a governmental award, and had been given the title of Honored Performer of the RSFSR. But we received the same vague replies from the Soviet bureaucracy: yes, a memorial to Messing should be erected, they said, but gave no further instructions to resolve the issue. What we needed was two thousand rubles, but even this wasn't the crux of the problem. It seemed that someone was persistently trying to foil our plans. We continued to storm the Ministry of Culture with inquiries, using famous and honored people to petition on our behalf. The last appeal was signed by several famous National Performers of the USSR. Still, no memorial was erected.

As a general rule, highly creative people leave behind material traces as well as memories of their work. Artists leave canvases, and composers leave their scores. Even the gardener leaves the inspired work of his hands, perhaps an apple tree or lilac bush he once planted.

But what kind of tangible trace is left behind by sorcerers, mediums, or psychics? What fruits are left behind by those whose creative gift is to see the invisible and hear the inaudible? What of their personal essence remains behind for us?

Even today, so many years after Wolf Messing's death, I cannot reconcile myself to such an injustice. He deserves to be remembered. I can only guess what power stood in the way of the justly deserved perpetuation of his memory — and the reasons why. It is possible that only Wolf knew the real reason, a secret he may have carried to the grave. My suspicions are based on one of our conversations which was filled with hints and innuendos.

Before his death, Wolf read and reread a letter he'd received from Israel telling about life there, and which he discussed with us. In the early 1970s the first small streams of Jews began to trickle out of the Soviet Union. A mutual acquaintance who was present asked Wolf why he himself didn't leave. Wolf glanced at me. "You know, she and Sasha will leave," he said, "and Sasha will work as a doctor somewhere in the northern United States. I told Tanya this on Sasha's tenth birthday. I know she didn't believe me then, and even now will deny it, saying she can't leave her mother and me as well. But we'll no longer be around. She'll leave in 1978. As for me, they'd sooner put me away than let me go."

Messing made these comments in a quiet and measured voice while gazing at the floor. He wouldn't say anything further and never brought up his feelings or prediction again. They had been pronounced in too solemn and serious a tone for me to pry for added information. He never specifically mentioned the possibility of receiving invitations from Israel, just as he had never talked of going even on a tourist excursion to Bulgaria, for example, or to his former homeland. (He loved Poland to his last day.) This struck me as peculiar; after all, Wolf had spent the first forty years of his life continually traveling overseas. I can't rule out the possibility that the key to the mystery is laying at the Lubyanka Prison, or even behind the Spassky gates of the Kremlin.

To be sure, Wolf Messing's prediction came true. In 1978 my son and I left our homeland and eventually settled in Detroit. I brought to the West only a few mementos of my friendship with Wolf Messing. While they are of no great artistic or intrinsic value, they mean everything to me. My son graduated from medical school in Ohio within two years, remaining there to work as a doctor and instructor. My adopted son, Vladimir, stayed in the Soviet Union.

Sometimes I feel like opening the doors of my buffet and getting out one of the two cups from which Wolf and his wife drank tea in Moscow. I want to fill it up with Lipton tea, to mix the past with the present! But I have to keep myself in check, for these china souvenirs — first editions from the Kuznetsov china factory, famous in Czarist Russia — are much too fragile. Having survived a flight across the ocean, they must wait for better times, perhaps when the name of their former owner brings them back from oblivion. I also have an Eskimo doll that watches me with its silk eyes — a gift to Messing from northern Russia. Near it I keep Messing's cigarette case, engraved with the inscription: "My dear friend Taibele, I am always with you. W. Messing, Moscow, March 27, 1967."

Occasionally I think I can still smell the nicotine stench of those detestable Kazbeks cigarettes, so I never open it. Let the Eskimo do this during the night, while people are asleep and fairy tales come to life.

In the same sideboard I keep the two books dearest to him: A. Vishnevsky's *A Surgeon's Diary* and N. Amosov's *Thoughts and the Heart*. At times I reverently stroke their dust jackets. What good fortune it was that I managed to preserve them and bring them with me; so many parcels I sent from Moscow were lost. The autographs in these volumes include tributes to Wolf that speak better than all my own words: "as a sign of wonderment and admiration of a miracle," wrote Nikolai Amosov. Could anything have said it better?

The wooden carving given to Messing by the Volga peasants has been preserved. I also managed to bring along several photographs: One is of the ring/talisman that disappeared after Wolf's death.

I said before that Messing left no living relatives, but we recently learned that a niece, Marta Messing, survived the Nazi concentration camps and escaped, along with some Russians, to Argentina, where she currently lives.

But back in the Soviet Union there are no relatives to whom his cemetery mound could be assigned. Therefore, this sad relic was issued to me:

CERTIFICATE OF REGISTRATION

ISSUED to Citizen T. L. Lungin
For registration of grave 4828 on plot No. 38
of W. G. Messing, deceased 11/08/74,
buried at the Vostryakov Cemetery.

Director of Cemetery — TLYAKHA
11/14/74
Vostryakov Bureau of
Interment Services

In 1981 I received wonderful news from Moscow. After waiting vainly seven years for the state to establish a memorial, Valentina Ivanovskaya and Aleksei themselves erected a black granite slab with a ceramic portrait of Wolf Messing.

Will I ever again be able to visit the grave of this man, who was so dear to me?

Index

A

Abel (neuropathologist), 55–56
About Myself (Messing), 6–7, 36
Abramov, Michael, 147
Academy of Science (USSR), 84
Agranenko, Victor, 150
Airline flights, 123–124
Aksakov, Alexander N., 102
Aleichem, Sholom, 35–36
Aleksei (W.M.'s friend), 194–195, 196, 200, 204
All Russian Congress of Psychoneurologists (1924), 10
Amosov, Nikolai, 188, 203
Andropov, Yuri, 85
Animal communication, 120, 121
Anti-Semitism, 28, 64, 148
Arrgo. *See* Levitin, L.C.
Artek (motion picture), 15–16
A. S. Popov Scientific-Technical Society for Radio Engineering, Electronics and Communications, 85

B

Bakulev Institute of Heart and Vascular Surgery, 174–175
Banker, hypnotized, 75–76
Barnard, Christiaan, 181
Ben Ali (fakir), 102
Berger, Hans, 91–92
Bersenev, Ivan N., 79
Blackmail, attempted, 65

Blindfolding, 115–116
Blokhin, Nikolai, 48–49
Braid, James, 126
Bukharin, Nikolai, 148
Burakovsky, Vladimir, 175, 190
Burdenko Clinic, 29, 31–32
Burdenko, Nikolai, 31–32
Busch Circus, 58
Butterflies, 120
Bux, Kuda, 92
Bykov, K.M., 89

C

Cagliostro, Count, 103–104
Carlson, Chester, 6
Catalepsy
   › of W.M., 9, 61, 97–98, 140
   › of yogis, 61, 97, 140
Central House of Medical Workers, 150
Charlatanry, 96–97, 102
Chavchavadze, Nina, 24
Chitashvili, Dick, 96
Chukovsky, Kornei I., 79
Clairvoyance, 121–122
Clairvoyance and Materialization (Galey), 100 (note)
Communist Party of the Soviet Union, Twentieth Congress of (1956), 101
Council of Ministers of the USSR, 83
Czartorysky family, 61–63

D

Davydovich, Alexander, 191
Dean, Douglas, 6
DeBakey, Michael, 176, 190, 193
Dreams, 136
Dumas, Alexander, 103

E

Einstein, Alfred, 59
Electroencephalography, 91, 105–106
Electromagnetic spectrum, 90
Electromagnetic wave theory, 106
European Messenger, 101
Experimental Research of Mental Suggestion (Vasiliev), 5
Eyeglasses, misplaced, 21

F

Fakery. *See* Charlatanry
Feuchtwanger, Lion, 69
Fifty Years in the Ranks (Ignatiev), 81–82
Fighter planes, 79
Folk medicine, 131
Fraud. *See* Charlatanry
Freud, Sigmund, 59, 99, 136
Frolova, Amonina Alekseevna, 48

G

Gagarin, Uri, 173
Gandhi, Mahatma, 61
Gausen (clairvoyant), 69
Gavrilov, Leopold, 143–145
Geley, Gustave, 100 (note)
Germany
› invades Russia, 18, 70, 78
› prophecies concerning, 11

Germonov, Mikhail, 158–160
Gestapo, 69–70
Goethe, Johann Wolfgang von, 99–100
Gorbachev, Mikhail, 148
Gorgius of Lentini, 93
Griboyedov, Alexander S., grave of, 23
Grizadubova, Valentina, 151
Guards
› German, 71
› Soviet, 77
Guzik, Jan, 100

H

Handwriting analysis, 99–100
Hannussen, Erik Jan, 103
Hertz, Heinrich, 90
Hitler, Adolf, 4, 11, 69, 77
Home, Daniel Dunglas, 101
Houdini, Harry, 100
Hypnotism, 126–132
› telepathic. *See* Telepathic hypnosis
Hypotaxia, 127–128

I

Ideomotor activity
› Soviet science and, 9, 89
› W.M. and, 109
Ignatiev, Aleksei, 81–82
Incest, Oedipal, 136–138
Indecent suggestions, 115–116
Institute of Diplomatic Relations, 107
Institute of Philosophy, 83
Institut Metapsychique International, 84

"In the World of Human Thought," 108–109
Iraida Mikhailovna, 27, 30, 47, 147, 152
› Aida and, 49, 52–53
› death of, 187
› operation on, 32–33
› Valentina Ivanovskaya and, 131
Ivanovskaya, Valentina Iosifovna, 53, 153, 191, 199
› at W.M.'s funeral, 194
› investigated, 197
› W.M.'s memorial and, 199, 205

J

Janos (Hungarian clown), 71

K

Kamensky, Yuri, 104
Kassirsky, Josef, 48, 145,146
Keldysh, Mstislav, 176, 190
KGB, 75, 84
Kitaygorodsky, Alexander, 87, 103, 105
Knoring, Oleg, 25
Kobak (manager), 60
Kogan, Ippolite, 104
Komarov, Vladimir, 177–178,
Kositsky G.I., 109–111, 115
Kovalev, Konstantin, 79
Kramova, Nadeshda Filipovna, 160–163
Krymsky, Leonid, 192
Kubansky, Polina, 96
Kuni, Mikhail, 159

L

Laboratory for Bio-Electronics, 86
Laboratory for Bio-Information, 85–86, 104
Lautenzack Brothers, The (Feuchtwanger), 69
Lazurkina, Darya, 101–102
Lenin Academy of Agricultural Sciences, 32
Leningrad, German siege of, 33–34
Lenin, Vladimir I., spirit of, 101–102
Levitin, L.C., 159
Lubyanka prison, 76
Lungin, Garrett, 165
Lungin, Iva, 165–166
Lungin, Sasha, 192
› birth of, 20
› career of, 202–203
› childhood of, 46
Lungin, Sasha (continued)
› education of, 142–145
› as fisherman, 155–156
› love life of, 154
› marriage of, 165–166
Lungin, Tatiana
› adopts Vladimir, 52
› meets W.M.
» in Moscow, 13–17
» in Tbilisi, 20–21
› moves to U.S., 202
› photojournalistic career of, 26–27
› radiation sickness of, 52–53, 145–146
Lungin, Tomash, 166

Lungin, Vladimir, 53, 142, 154, 203
Lysenko, Trofim D., 32

M

Man and the Universe (Vasiliev),
  94
Marxist materialism, 84
Mendeleyev, Dimitry I., 101
Mental Suggestion at a Distance
  (Vasiliev), 91–92
Mesmer, Franz Anton, 127
Messing, Aida Mikhailovna,
  88, 158
› death of, 50–52
› illness of, 27, 49–51
› meets Lungin, 21
› meets W.M., 82
Messing, Marta, 204
Messing, Wolf
› *About Myself*, 6–7, 35
› after death of Aida, 52–53
› anniversary performance
  (1966), 150–152
› arrested by Gestapo, 69–70
› in Berlin, 41–42, 56–57
› brain of, 192
› childhood "vision" of, 37–38
› death of, 191
› during WWII, 79–82
› early years of, 32–46, 57–67
› errors of, 175–177
› escape to Russia, 72–73
› funeral of, 192–194
› hospitalized, 186
  » for appendicitis, 150
  » for blood circulation
    obstruction, 189
  » for obliterating
    endarteritis, 171

» for tumor, 43
› hypnotism and, 41, 126–132
› instructions given to, 118–120
› life principles of, 63, 79
› meets Aida, 82
› meets Lungin
  » in Moscow, 13–18
  » in Tbilisi, 20
› meets Stalin, 74
› memorial for, 202, 205
› pets of, 27
› possessions of, 200–201, 204
› as psychologist, 133–139
› religion of, 30, 37–39
› residence of, 27
› seventieth birthday
  celebration, 154
› sins of, 41
› Upper Volga vacation of,
  154–156
Mihalasky, John, 6
Ministry of Culture, 82
Money, stolen, 122–123
Morality, 130
Mostorg, 122
Murders, solved, 178, 181–182

N

National Performance
  Bureau, 44
Newark College of Engineering, 6
Nikolaev, Karl, 104
Nikulin, Uri, 195
NKVD, 76

O

Occultism. *See* Spiritualism
Organ transplants, 180–181

P

Pakhomova, Lydia, 140
Panoptikum (Berlin), 56
Paranoid delusion, 134–136
"Parapsychology:
    Fiction or Reality?", 84
Parapsychology
  › Soviet, 83
  › Vasiliev and, 84–85
Parapsychology Conference,
    First Annual International
    (Moscow: 1968), 7
Passover feast, 29
Pavlov, Ivan, 87, 88, 98, 111
  › on catalepsy, 98
  › Kositsky and, 111
Petefi, Shandora, 138
Petrovsky, Boris, 44
Pheromones, 120
Physical Society
    (St. Petersburg), 102
Pifelo (chiromancer), 98
Pigeon delusion, 135–136
Pilsudski, Josef, 75
Pokrovsky, Anatoly
    Vladimirovich, 190, 192
Ponomarenko, Pateleymon
    Kondratyevich, 73
Poskrebychev, Alexander, 74
Prater Amusement Park
    (Vienna), 58
Prostitution ring, Argentine, 64
Psyche (Berger), 91
Psychological emergencies, 133–139

R

Rapoport, Aida Mikhailovna. *See*
    Messing, Aida Mikhailovna

Rebus, 102
Relativity, theory of, 132
Religion
  › in Soviet Union, 28
  › of W.M., 28, 39–41
Rozhdestvensky, Robert, 94
Russian Society for
    Experimental Psychology, 102

S

Safonov, Vladimir, 113–114
Schiller-Shkolnik
    (psychographologist), 98
Schmidt (psychiatrist), 56
Science, Soviet, 82, 85, 88–93
Sechenov, I. M., 88, 109–112, 142
Sensory cuing.
    See Ideomotor activity
Sergeev (professor), 140–141
Shkolnik. *See* Schiller-Shkolnik
    (psychographologist)
Social classes, Soviet, 148
Somnambulism, 128
Soviet-Chinese border dispute,
    141–142
Soyuzdetfilm, 15
Spiritualism, 99–102
"Sportlotto," 168
Spy, German, 180
Stalin, Joseph
  › death of, 148
  › ESP and, 5
  › Leningrad siege and, 36
  › meets W.M., 74–75
  › telegram to W.M., 79
  › telepathic hypnosis and, 5
  › tolerates W.M., 42, 148
Stigmata, 93
Subliminal perception, 105

Surgeon's Diary, a (Vishnevsky), 188, 203
Suspended animation.
  See Catalepsy
Svinka-Zielinski, Ludmila, 6–7

T

Telepathic hypnosis, 9–10
  › of banker, 75
  › of ticket taker, 39, 129
Telepathy
  › A.S. Popov Society and, 86
  › of border guard, 108–109
  › Soviet science and, 88–94
Thoughts and the Heart (Amosov), 187, 203
Ticket taker, hypnotized, 42, 129
Tolstoy, Aleksei, 79
Tolstoy, Leo, 103
Toothache, 131

U

University of London Council for Psychical Investigations, 92

V

Vasiliev, Leonid L., 12, 91–92
  › *Experimental Research of Mental Suggestion*, 5
  › hypnotism and, 127
  › parapsychological studies and, 85
  › telepathic hypnosis and, 5
Vasiliev, Mikhail, 94
Vavilov, Nikolai I., 32
Verne, Jules, 132
Vestnik Evropy, 101

Vishnevsky, Alexander Alexandrovich, 171, 186, 187

W

Walk in Torment (A. Tolstoy), 80
Warsaw Circus, 102
Wells, H.G., 94
"White Veil, The" (Petefi), 138
Wintergarten (Berlin), 57
World War II
  › prophecies concerning, 5–11
  › in Russia, 18–24, 79–82

Y

Yefim (illusionist), 96
Yogis, 9, 61, 97, 140
Yaroshevsky, M.G., 83, 87–88
Yuzef (murder victim), 179

Z

Zellmeister (manager), 56, 60
Zhukovsky (lieutenant-general), 175–176
Zielinski, Ludmila Svinka.
  See Svinka-Zielinski, Ludmila

Glagoslav Publications Catalogue

- *The Time of Women* by Elena Chizhova
- *Sin* by Zakhar Prilepin
- *Hardly Ever Otherwise* by Maria Matios
- *The Lost Button* by Irene Rozdobudko
- *Khatyn* by Ales Adamovich
- *Christened with Crosses* by Eduard Kochergin
- *The Vital Needs of the Dead* by Igor Sakhnovsky
- *METRO 2033* (Dutch Edition) by Dmitry Glukhovsky
- *METRO 2034* (Dutch Edition) by Dmitry Glukhovsky
- *A Poet and Bin Laden* by Hamid Ismailov
- *Asystole* by Oleg Pavlov
- *Kobzar* by Taras Shevchenko
- *White Shanghai* by Elvira Baryakina
- *The Stone Bridge* by Alexander Terekhov
- *King Stakh's Wild Hunt* by Uladzimir Karatkevich
- *Depeche Mode* by Serhii Zhadan
- *Saraband Sarah's Band* by Larysa Denysenko
- *Herstories*, An Anthology of New Ukrainian Women Prose Writers
- *Watching The Russians* (Dutch Edition) by Maria Konyukova
- *The Hawks of Peace* by Dmitry Rogozin
- *The Grand Slam and Other Stories* (Dutch Edition) by Leonid Andreev
- *The Battle of the Sexes Russian Style* by Nadezhda Ptushkina
- *A Book Without Photographs* by Sergei Shargunov

More coming soon...

www.ingramcontent.com/pod-product-compliance
Lightning Source LLC
Chambersburg PA
CBHW030147310326
41914CB00087B/196